JOHN STEINBECK
THE YEARS OF GREATNESS, 1936–1939

Edited by Tetsumaro Hayashi
With an Introduction by
John H. Timmerman

Derived from papers presented by the North American delegates at the Third International Steinbeck Congress held in May 1990 in Honolulu, Hawaii—under the cosponsorship of the Steinbeck Society of Japan and the International Steinbeck Society—these ten essays, arranged in two parts, seek to provide a clearer understanding of Steinbeck's critical years of greatness.

Part I discusses Steinbeck's women with special emphasis on the function of the feminine from original perspectives by using the latest research sources, including some of the Steinbeck-Gwyn love letters and poems. Part II explores the Depression trilogy—*In Dubious Battle, Of Mice and Men*, and *The Grapes of Wrath*—Steinbeck's major works of the late 1930s.

Taken as a whole, these ten captivating, entertaining, readable, and rewarding essays,

(continued on the back flap)

JOHN STEINBECK

JOHN STEINBECK
THE YEARS OF GREATNESS, 1936–1939

Edited by
Tetsumaro Hayashi

with an Introduction by
John H. Timmerman

THE UNIVERSITY OF ALABAMA PRESS

TUSCALOOSA & LONDON

Copyright © 1993
The University of Alabama Press
Tuscaloosa, Alabama 35487–0380
All rights reserved
Manufactured in the United States of America

The paper on which this book is printed meets the minimum requirements of
American National Standard for Information Science-Permanence of Paper for
Printed Library Materials, ANSI Z39.48-1984.

Library of Congress Cataloging-in-Publication Data

John Steinbeck : the years of greatness, 1936–1939 / edited by
Tetsumaro Hayashi
p.   cm.
Papers presented by the North American delegates to the Third International
Steinbeck Congress, held in Honolulu, Hawaii, May 27–30, 1991.
Includes bibliographical references (p.) and index.
ISBN 0-8173-0692-7 (alk. paper)
1. Steinbeck, John, 1902–1968—Criticism and interpretation—
Congresses.   I. Hayashi, Tetsumaro.

PS3537.T3234Z7156   1993
813'.52—dc20   93-3696

To
Yasuo Hashiguchi,
Kiyoshi Nakayama,
and
Shigeharu Yano,
who made the Third International
Steinbeck Congress possible

Contents

Preface

John Steinbeck: The Years of Greatness derives from the North American delegates' lectures and papers presented at the Third International Steinbeck Congress, held in Honolulu, Hawaii, May 27–30, 1991, under the sponsorship of the Steinbeck Society of Japan in collaboration with the International John Steinbeck Society. The meeting was a memorable occasion for attending Steinbeck scholars and enthusiasts. It was a chance, first of all, to enjoy the generosity and hospitality of President Yasuo Hashiguchi, Professors Kiyoshi Nakayama, Shigeharu Yano, Hisashi Egusa, and Takahiko Sugiyama, and the officers and volunteers of the Steinbeck Society of Japan, who went out of their way to make us feel welcome. It was an opportunity, as well, to confirm our faith in the value of collaboration, encouragement, and the mutual exchange of ideas through such international gatherings.

Because many members of the Steinbeck Society were unable to attend, I began compiling the North American papers in one volume in order to make them available to a larger audience. The resulting collection is a partial but logical sequel to *John Steinbeck: East and West* (Steinbeck Monograph Series, no. 8, 1978), edited by myself, Yasuo Hashiguchi, and Richard F. Peterson and based on the papers presented at the First International Steinbeck Congress, held in Japan. (We have also published the proceedings of the Second International Congress, held in Salinas, California, in 1984, *John Steinbeck: From Salinas to the World*, eds. Shigeharu Yano, *et al.* [Tokyo: Gaku Shobo Press, 1986]). The Steinbeck Society of Japan, under the joint editorship of Professors Kiyoshi Nakayama, Scott Pugh, and Shigeharu Yano, has published the Asian papers as a book, *John Steinbeck: Asian Perspectives* (Osaka, Japan: Osaka Kyoiku Tosho Co., Ltd., 1992).

Now, with the memory of one of the most exhilarating Steinbeck gatherings ever held still fresh in our minds, we move into the third decade of our society's exploration into Steinbeck's enigmatic, magical literature, having had our courage, resourcefulness, and vitality renewed.

Tetsumaro Hayashi, Editor
Muncie, Indiana
U.S.A.

Acknowledgments

To John Steinbeck, who has inspired all of us contributors to learn, to teach, and to write; to those who participated in the Third International Steinbeck Congress held in the Nobel Prize laureate's honor; to Mrs. Elaine Steinbeck, the Estate of John Steinbeck, and Mr. Eugene H. Winick and Ms. Julie Fallowfield of McIntosh and Otis, for permission to quote from Steinbeck; and to Penguin Books USA and Ms. Florence B. Eichin for permission to quote from Steinbeck's three major Depression novels, I want to extend my sincere appreciation.

To the staff of The University of Alabama Press, especially Nicole Mitchell, Acquisitions Editor, and Malcolm M. Mac-Donald, Director, I am grateful for their professionalism, and to all the scholars who evaluated the manuscript, I am grateful for their expert advice.

To the contributors I owe my sincere gratitude for their cooperation, friendship, and support. To my secretaries, Ms. Michelle L. Hunt and Ms. Stephanie E. Ponder, who have with infinite patience and goodwill typed, retyped, and revised the manuscript, and to Ms. Tera L. Miles, Mrs. Cathy D. Stewart, and Dr. Beverly K. Sampson, who helped me proofread the manuscript in various stages, I extend profound thanks. I am also grateful to my Ball State University sponsors—Dr. C. Warren Vander Hill, Dr. Donald E. Van Meter, Dr. Charles L. Houck, Dr. Linda K. Hanson, and Mr. Thomas E. Spangler—for generously supporting my work as codirector of the Third International Steinbeck Congress and as editor of the proceedings of the North American papers, which evolved into this book.

Tetsumaro Hayashi

Permissions

1. The Estate of John Steinbeck granted permission to the various contributors to quote from Steinbeck's writings throughout the essays in *John Steinbeck: The Years of Greatness*. We gratefully thank Mr. Eugene H. Winick, president of McIntosh and Otis, Inc., for permission, as well as Ms. Julie Fallowfield for permission for Professor Robert DeMott's quotations.

2. Penguin Books USA, Inc., granted us permission to use quotations from the following works in this book:

(A.) From *The Grapes of Wrath* by John Steinbeck (© 1939, renewed © 1967 by John Steinbeck. Used by permission of Viking Penguin, a division of Penguin Books USA, Inc.)

(B.) From *Of Mice and Men* by John Steinbeck (© 1937, renewed © 1965 by John Steinbeck. Used by permission of Viking Penguin, a division of Penguin Books USA, Inc.)

(C.) From *In Dubious Battle* by John Steinbeck (© 1936, renewed © 1964 by John Steinbeck. Used by permission of Viking Penguin, a division of Penguin Books USA, Inc.) We gratefully thank Ms. Florence B. Eichin, Permissions Manager of Penguin Books USA, Inc., for permissions.

INTRODUCTION

JOHN H. TIMMERMAN

Power and Grace
The Shape of a Tradition

It is the task of one who introduces a volume of essays to provide some chart, some road map, to the course of arguments presented. Something of that road map will be provided here, of course. It is also worth a moment's reflection to consider the value of this collection as a whole. Two qualities, it seems to me, typify these contributions and thereby grant the collection its stellar quality.

Seldom have I found gathered in one volume a group of essays so entertaining, so readable, and so rewarding as these. Although varied in style and subject matter, collectively they form one of the best pieces of expository prose I have had opportunity to linger over in some time.

I did linger, at times to savor the peculiar beauty and force of a particular phrasing, but also to savor ideas. Despite the amount of Steinbeck criticism in recent years, these essays do not merely beat about the same old ideas, trying to squeeze a bit more ink out of depleted resources. They represent investigations by scholars who are thinking in inventive, crisp ways.

They enjoy their thinking. They take risks. They speculate daringly, but with a hard armor of resources, sound argument, and rhetorical verve.

If freshness, vigor, and lucidity of style and approach constitute the first quality of excellence in these essays, thoroughness of investigative research constitutes the second. The essays bear evidence of uncommon research energy. By no means do they simply offer speculative "angles of critical vision" upon the same old problems. Rather, they continually bear evidence of imaginative and determined literary detective work. Investigations into Steinbeck's personal and literary life and research into cultural and literary conditions of his time have produced telling new materials. The amount and quality of original research make these essays, quite simply, indispensable additions to the knowledge of Steinbeck's work and the culture of the late 1930s.

Part I: The Years of Greatness: Steinbeck's Women

Both tone and quality of this book are established by John Ditsky's "'Your Own Mind Coming Out in the Garden': Steinbeck's Elusive Woman." Ditsky's study, one of several essays in the collection concerned with gender roles in Steinbeck's fiction, focuses particularly upon female characters in *The Long Valley*. The essay, however, goes beyond an examination of the roles of women in these stories. It also examines Steinbeck's creativity itself in gender terms: "Ultimately, Steinbeck's elusive and remarkable Woman is the work herself."

Ditsky's provocative essay provides solid entrance into the

collection, for while it is rooted in careful research and critical analysis, it also speculates daringly. Ditsky holds several strings of argument in tension throughout the essay, then ties them neatly together at the conclusion in a way that both convinces and challenges us with fresh insights into Steinbeck's creative process.

From a concern with fictional women in Steinbeck's work, Robert DeMott turns our attention to a historical woman in "After *The Grapes of Wrath*: A Speculative Essay on John Steinbeck's Suite of Love Poems for Gwyn, 'The Girl of the Air.'" DeMott traces the historical composition of this grouping of twenty-five love poems written for Gwendolyn Conger and never published or made public in independent format. The poems were written surreptitiously in a pocket-size notebook during a tumultuous courtship in 1940, prior to Steinbeck's 1943 divorce from Carol and his marriage eleven days later to Gwyn.

"Obviously, there will always be lacunae to be filled in a writer's life," writes DeMott early in his essay. Few such lacunae in Steinbeck's life are more intriguing than his courtship of Gwyn, particularly with the testimony—often truculent, self-aggrandizing, and romanticized—she left in her memoir, "The Closest Witness." But that memoir also turned up a streak of biographical ore that DeMott mines to perfection, for while the holograph copy of the suite of poems is sealed against public perusal, the memoirs include the twenty-five poems.

It is one thing to locate such a treasure trove, but quite another to know what to do with it. DeMott knows. Not only does he quote large sections from the poems, essentially made public for the first time in this essay, but he also expertly relates the poems to Steinbeck's life—his activities, longings, and aspirations—and to his literary career and themes.

Two additional essays in Part I grapple with the role of female characters in Steinbeck's fiction. Both illuminate the nature of the fictional work as a whole by means of the particularized discussion.

In "Looking at Lisa: The Function of the Feminine in Steinbeck's *In Dubious Battle*," Abby Werlock demonstrates how a new insight into a supposedly minor character can sharpen and deepen our understanding of the work as a whole. This point seems to be particularly true of Steinbeck's fiction, where rather quiet and unobtrusive characters often attain a position of thematic significance in a work. One such character is Lisa of *In Dubious Battle*.

Such an analysis in itself is meritorious, for Lisa's character is richer than the casual reader might perceive. But Werlock also points out how the humanity of other characters—Mac, Jim, and Doc in particular—is determined by their relationship with Lisa, and how the "quiet power" of the woman functions throughout the novel.

Another powerful, but indeed quiet and sometimes quite indistinct, female character from the fiction of this period is the haunting figure of Curley's wife in *Of Mice and Men*. In 1938, at the instigation of Annie Laurie Williams, Steinbeck wrote a character sketch of Curley's wife for Claire Luce, who was performing in the role during the New York run of *Of Mice and Men*. Although intended to clear up some of Luce's misgivings about representing the character, Steinbeck's sketch actually outlined the moral nature of Curley's wife rather than providing concrete details for stage direction. But that letter was only one stage in the remarkable run of Steinbeck's play and the shaping of the character of Curley's wife. In "The Dialogic Tension in Steinbeck's Portrait of

Curley's Wife," Charlotte Hadella uses Mikhail M. Bakhtin's "dialogic tension" approach to examine Steinbeck's attitude toward and fictional use of the character. Hadella also traces the development of the character of Curley's wife as a mythic type.

Part II: The Years of Greatness: Steinbeck's Worker Trilogy

The second part of this collection represents a variety of critical approaches to Steinbeck's work. And his work responds well to the varied methodologies, for while he achieved renown as a storyteller, the stories he told were inevitably rooted in human histories, aspirations, conflicts, and philosophical constructs.

Louis Owens's "Writing 'in Costume': The Missing Voices in *In Dubious Battle*" immediately sets the tone with a provocative analysis of Steinbeck's and Carlos Bulosan's differing perspectives on the Filipino worker in California labor. Intrigued by Bulosan's passing comment about Caldwell and Steinbeck—"Why did they write in costume?"—Owens sets for himself the task of discovering exactly what Bulosan had in mind. His detective work produces a number of fascinating surprises. For example, he finds a series of curious parallels between Bulosan and Jim Nolan. More significant, however, are the ways Steinbeck manipulated history to suit his artistic aims. There are, for example, no Filipino workers identified as such in the novel, whereas in historical fact Filipinos (as Steinbeck surely knew, having worked with them on the Spreckels Ranch during the 1920s) were actively involved in labor organization. In fact, Steinbeck's fictionalized strike,

Owens demonstrates, was quite at odds with the ones that were actually a part of Bulosan's experience. How does one account for Steinbeck's rendition, his manipulation of historical fact? Owens turns his attention to Steinbeck's narrative technique, using Mikhail M. Bakhtin's concept of "double-voiced discourse" to explain the rhetorical effect of the novel and its intentional irony.

From Owens's study of the particularized history of the Filipino worker and Steinbeck's rhetorical strategy in *In Dubious Battle*, Thomas Tammaro broadens our perspective of the book by placing it in the genre of working-class novels. "Sharing Creation: Steinbeck, *In Dubious Battle*, and the Working-Class Novel in American Literature" does more than identify the novel as a generic entity, however. Tammaro also sets before us an evincive argument for inclusion of the working-class novel in the curriculum. "An understanding of the working-class experience in America," he argues, "is crucial to our understanding of the American experience." Yet such novels are seriously underrepresented in the canon of American literature. *In Dubious Battle,* in Tammaro's estimation, is a primary candidate to "fill this vacuum and address this reluctance to read and study a literature that has too long been ignored and is too central to our common experience."

That Ed Ricketts was both Steinbeck's closest friend and also prototype for many of his fictional characters is a standard in Steinbeck criticism. Just how far, though, did this friendship and this prototype influence Steinbeck's fiction? In "Reflections of Doc: The Persona of Ed Ricketts in *Of Mice and Men*," Thomas Fensch ponders that question, stimulated anew by a conversation he had with Pauline Pearson, who claimed that Ricketts's influence appears in "book after book by Steinbeck." Fensch makes a case for Slim, the "jerkline driver," as a representative of Ed Ricketts in *Of Mice and Men*. However, the influence extends beyond character type to the narrative point of view Steinbeck adopts as representative of Ricketts's philosophy.

Such critical, analytic studies provide us with new insights for considering both the texts and their contexts. Furthermore, they deepen our understanding of the work by focusing attention upon characters and thematic patterns easily overlooked in a casual reading. In "Tell Again, George," Robert Morsberger, whose work with Steinbeck's career in film has been both authoritative and profound, examines the history of *Of Mice and Men* as a stage and film work.

Beginning with a precise and thorough review of Steinbeck's technique for writing a novelette and a play simultaneously, Morsberger sets forth a careful history of *Of Mice and Men* as a staged and filmed production. He smoothly incorporates critical reviews of the productions, permitting us to relive the historical process. The revisions that Steinbeck worked through in the adaptation to the stage, moreover, give us a sense of his craftsmanship as a dramatist. The wealth of details, from costs of production to analysis of musical scores, marks this immaculately researched study as one of the central essays for a complete understanding of the literary history of *Of Mice and Men*.

Mimi Gladstein, to whom John Ditsky dedicated his contribution, is a much admired scholar, not just for the vigor of her critical insights, her pioneering work in feminist studies, and her wit and clarity of style, but also for the way she shapes her critical analyses as stories. These never fail to quicken the interest of readers or listeners and allow them, finally, to appropriate the stories as their own. All these qualities are much in evidence in her essay, "*The Grapes of Wrath*:

Steinbeck and the Eternal Immigrant." Gladstein weaves into the story of the immigrant—the historical but also the archetypal immigrant—her father's story as an immigrant to America, which is finally also Gladstein's story.

Certainly Steinbeck invites this insight. Having written that *The Grapes of Wrath* is "a five-layered book," Steinbeck added that "a reader will find as many as he can and won't find more than he has in himself." If the book is about homelessness, exploitation, and exodus, Gladstein writes, then "it is also the story of the quintessential American experience," and we as readers are constantly rediscovering ourselves in the experience of the book. Gladstein's approach toward this rediscovery is to develop parallels between the Joad family's exodus and the immigrant experience.

When *The Grapes of Wrath* was first published, it was met with resistance and censorship. Although some of the denunciations in Oklahoma and Texas, because issued through legislative action, are notorious, the resistance in California was equally fierce. In California, however, it was unique in that it prompted several revisionistic literary rebuttals. These attempted at once to denigrate Steinbeck's novel and to exonerate the landowners of the state. In "California Answers *The Grapes of Wrath*," Susan Shillinglaw examines some of these dubious literary efforts.

Through her careful research, moreover, Shillinglaw demonstrates the importance of the person behind the work. What kinds of historical experience and perspective, for example, motivated the ideological perspectives of Ruth Comfort Mitchell's *Of Human Kindness*, or Frank Taylor's articles on the landowners' work ethic? How does Marshall Hartranft's career in real estate color his *Grapes of Gladness*? A scholar is obligated, by virtue of the very nature of Steinbeck's work, to exercise a certain amount of historical criticism. Shillinglaw convincingly employs historical methodologies, locating the works countering Steinbeck's reading of history in their own cultural positions. It is a provocative essay, unraveling and reconstructing the historical detritus of a collision of ideologies and idealisms. In addition to enriching our understanding of the reaction of certain groups in California to *The Grapes of Wrath*, Shillinglaw's study ultimately brings to life the entire cultural, historical milieu of the novel itself.

The late 1930s, the historical frame for this collection of essays, represents one of the high points in Steinbeck's artistic career. It was then that he emerged from an incubatory period as a struggling regional writer and exploded into a period of international renown. The creative outpouring did more than simply wash over his readers; it immersed them in story and changed the way they viewed others and themselves. The power of that creative force has not diminished in its effects. The essays of this collection capture the genius of that creative power, examine it, learn from it, and set forth, in the new creative power of the critical act, fresh ways for us as modern readers to view the works, others, and ourselves.

Part I

The Years of Greatness
Steinbeck's Women

1

JOHN DITSKY

"Your Own Mind Coming Out in the Garden"

Steinbeck's Elusive Woman

for Mimi Reisel Gladstein

During the period in which John Steinbeck wrote the three Depression novels that are the special focus of this Third International Steinbeck Congress, he also published one other notable volume of fiction: the memorable assemblage of short stories collectively entitled *The Long Valley*.[1] Few readers or critics of Steinbeck would argue with the claim that these four volumes represent Steinbeck at his best. But as Robert S. Hughes, Jr., noted in his paper for the Tenth Salinas Steinbeck Festival in August 1989,[2] there are very different orientations in Steinbeck's short fiction as opposed to his novels, with the differences being bridged perhaps only in the hybrid work *The Pastures of Heaven*. Moreover, little of *The Long Valley* has anything to do with the struggles of the American worker, the preoccupation of the novels that are our subject.

Tetsumaro Hayashi, our director, originally suggested a

paper on Steinbeck criticism as it is today and as it will be in the future. But I feel I exhausted my powers as sage and guru when I did much the same sort of thing in 1988 at the Ninth Salinas Steinbeck Festival. And the future of Steinbeck criticism is rapidly passing into younger hands that have no need of my powers of prophecy. I would therefore like to speak about parts of *The Long Valley* in a way that expands upon the observations I made in Salinas in 1988, and also springs from some of what I had to say in the same city a year later. In so doing, I would like to try to pin down some of the characteristic means by which Steinbeck, as though he were a writer of detective fiction, made a lifelong quest of understanding that elusive thing called Woman—and perhaps, like most of us, failed.

The most prominent of Steinbeck's feminist critics is certainly Mimi Reisel Gladstein, who has written with conviction about Steinbeck's "indestructible" females, as well as about the apparent "misogyny" *The Wayward Bus* evidences.[3] More recently, she has also written about the curious anomaly by which Steinbeck, who knew so many remarkable women in his life, fails to recreate them in his own fiction.[4] Gladstein fairly admits that the autonomy of the artist includes the right to do precisely that if he chooses, but she just as rightly raises the issue of the peculiarity of the situation. The Depression novels clearly prove that Steinbeck's depiction of events on the picket lines and at the hiring tables does not reflect the "actual" presence of charismatic women at those scenes in the "real" 1930s. With the classic exception of the "indestructible" Ma Joad, the women in *In Dubious Battle, Of Mice and Men,* and *The Grapes of Wrath* are apt to be either sad or silly—or both. But in *The Long Valley,* as Susan Shillinglaw has recently been proving, women—or the Woman—come into their own, albeit a bit at a time.[5] That this quest for the nature of Woman occupied Steinbeck for a lifetime is a subject beyond the scope of this chapter. That certain key stories in *The Long Valley* speak to the issue is what I intend to address.

In the three labor novels being discussed during this congress, the world of action is the world of men, with the women surrendering their relative passivity only in the third volume of the trilogy, if we can call it that, *The Grapes of Wrath*. There, it is true, Ma's assumption of the "male" function of action does come to represent the potential for revolutionary change in the human family, but its highest and most notorious achievement is the closing tableau, in which revolutionary action can also be said to be passion of a sort. Indeed, what Rose of Sharon participates in is a curious kind of act of love that has reminded some readers, myself included, of the results of another Passion, the biblical one, in its culmination in a version of the Pietà.[6] Woman here has not yet succeeded in moving out of her mythical and archetypal role; rather, she has simply stretched it a bit.

Hughes pointed out in Salinas that while the novels focus on society, the short stories deal with individual psychology. It is in the short stories, then, that we might expect to see women portrayed as individuals, whether or not they are confined there to doing the womanly appropriate things. In a recent issue of the *Steinbeck Quarterly*, I discuss one of the stories from *The Long Valley*, "The Murder," in which Woman is truly presented as the unfathomable Other, with her nearly species difference conveyed by Jelka's being a member of the Slavic race.[7] I also suggest that there is ambiguity in "The Murder" over whether Jim Moore's point of view, in its failure to understand womankind, is not also characteristic of Steinbeck himself. It may be significant that the last two stories in *The Long Valley* before the "Red Pony" pieces deal in a way with womankind: "The Murder," with its aforementioned ambiguities; and "St. Katy the Virgin," which I am not for a moment going to risk considering as a commentary on the female sex—though I did wake up in the middle of the night recently with the troubling question of whether St. Katy, that nasty little porker, might at least subconsciously have served as the model for Cathy Ames.

I

I am not about to deal with those stories in which Steinbeck may be throwing up his hands at the impossibility of understanding women, any more than I wish to deal with the symbolic implications of the collection's title, which just may allude to the existence of a patient, everlasting, and naturally female *place* where Man—male horse, male rider—thinks he is free to act. I want to deal with those three of the first four stories in the collection that attempt to answer the question "What is Woman?": "The Chrysanthemums," "The White Quail," and "The Snake." These stories have been extensively analyzed before, and I do not expect to be able to do much that is truly novel with them here, but perhaps I will be able to glean something from them that can take our thinking in a new direction.

Many of us have written about "The Chrysanthemums," surely the most often anthologized of Steinbeck's pieces, but few of us have wholly agreed. Like the other stories under consideration today, its ambiguities are centered in the mystery of Woman herself, but unlike the others, it pretends to a sympathy the others do not possess. Interestingly, however, what might strike a male reader as Steinbeck's most "feminist" piece of fiction does not seem to evoke the same response among women. In a recent class of mine, the women were deeply divided over the issue of whether Elisa Allen is a sympathetic figure or not. It would seem that more than half a century after the writing of "The Chrysanthemums," women are impatient with a character who appears to be unable or unwilling to do anything about her own perceived state of entrapment.

But Elisa's entrapment is deeply rooted in character, and her psychology is complicated by the fact that she both dresses and addresses her work in her garden in a mannish fashion. Furthermore, in her encounter with the tinker, it is the freedom of his man's life on the road that appeals to her as much as, if not more than, his maleness. I have written recently about the theatricality of this story,[8] and I would extend my remarks now by observing that Elisa is manipulated by the tinker into playing the female role, finding him some work to do and thus catering to his maleness, before he will complete the pretended transaction by accepting her unwanted flowers—which he, of course, abandons heartlessly. It is on the strength of this bit of dramatic self-delusion that Elisa indulges in her narcissistic cleansing, admiring, and adorning of her body. Her bewildered husband, Henry, noting the results, inadvertently but accurately describes them as "a kind of play." But he also describes what he sees as "strong," a curious term to use to describe a woman in the full flush of womanhood—that is, a woman fully possessed of stereotypical womanliness. Elisa is enough of a person by this time—a woman with a man's sense of freedom—that she can even consider going with Henry to the fights, and one can only guess what rewards poor Henry might have reaped later had she indeed gone. But only moments after the not-unexpected finding of the discarded chrysanthemums along the road, Elisa subsides into a state of "crying weakly—

like an old woman." It is a tribute to the perceptiveness of Steinbeck's presentation of the equivocal nature of human sexuality to note that after half a century or more, we have not by any means run out of things to say about this little story.

But no single Steinbeck story is able to express the ambiguities of the writer's attitudes towards Woman. Her mysteriousness would remain largely unfathomable to him until, perhaps, quite late in his career. To enlarge upon a point made earlier, we remember that Steinbeck's greatest novel ends with an awestruck visit to a shrine to femaleness, and that the book's last word is "mysteriously," referring to Rose of Sharon's smile.[9] The mystery of femaleness presented in "The Chrysanthemums" is approached from another angle in "The White Quail." Again, the female character is so preoccupied with her long-planned garden that she chooses her husband on the basis of whether or not the garden will "like" him (*TLV*, p. 28). When her choice lights on Harry Teller, her beauty makes him "hungry," but access to her "untouchable" nature depends on his compliant acceptance of the importance of her garden to her, for he recognizes—in the line which is the title of this paper—that the garden is the expression of her psychology (p. 29). But her mind, when it comes "out in the garden," is a curious one indeed, for she talks about the garden "almost as though she were talking about herself," and yet when she refers to a particular fuchsia tree—part of the garden that is herself—she calls it "he" (p. 31). This "he" is meant to protect the garden from intrusion from the wild world without; "pretty" Mary is not bothered by the process of destroying "slugs and snails" for her garden's sake, and she is willing to poison an intruding cat to preserve what is meant to be a bird sanctuary (pp. 31–32). Harry wonders what is going on inside her "cool, collected mind," but Mary indicates that she may not be what he thinks he sees; indeed, when she looks indoors from outside one evening, she finds herself "seeing" herself through the window, and she admires what she sees—and also the ability to appreciate her doubleness (pp. 33–34). But she cannot reveal herself to Harry on this score, for that would ruin things; her mind is as spoilable as her garden.

The secret garden of Mary's mind is thus preserved from infiltration in the same way she withholds her body from Harry when he cannot understand her attempts to prettify his man's world of business ethics. Later, when Harry has the temerity to crave an Irish terrier puppy, Mary's "curse of imagination" causes her to become feverish with a psychosomatic headache. One notes here, and with interest, the connecting of the power to imagine with the sexuality of the female, even to the extent of punishment by denial of sex—not to mention the proverbial headache that accompanies the denial, if not as part of the same incident then at least as part of the same page of narrative (*TLV*, p. 36).

One dusk, which Mary considers her "really-garden-time," a "little white hen quail" appears in her garden, and Mary immediately concludes—rather remarkably—that the quail is "like the essence of me, an essence boiled down to utter purity" (*TLV*, p. 38). The quail brings Mary memories of a ritual three "ecstasies," a sequence of moments in which her imagination stood poised on the threshold of experiences new to her: candy she mustn't taste, praise for her patience "like a gentian," and news of her father's death (p. 39). Mary's inhumanly protracted "purity," embodied in the quail, is next seen as threatened by a cat, and Harry's refusal to use poison against "animals in my garden" brings on predictable results: the headache, the locked bedroom door. Harry promises to shoot the cat with his air rifle to scare it off and thus protect what Mary calls "the secret me that no one can ever get at" (p. 41). Instead, he kills the quail, of course, though he tells himself he just wanted to scare it away, and he buries it outside the garden. Interestingly, the story switches focus at its ending to Harry; having killed his wife's "secret me," he blames himself and bemoans his loneliness.

Mary Teller can be called a pathological, grown child or what you will, but the salient fact of her story's narration is that it changes sides. At its ending, the male figure accepts his fate: he will never get inside his wife's mind and soul, and the story has already suggested that his access to her body may be at an end. The otherness of Woman has been confirmed again, as mystified men are left outside the garden with the unruly elements of existence: cats, dogs, horses, and tinker's dams. The balance of empathy seems to have shifted: the last words of "The Chrysanthemums" are "old woman," but those of "The White Quail" are a man's wailed "I'm so lonely!" (TLV, p. 42). The stories tally, however, in terms of the presentation of Woman as mysteriously possessed of the ability to order the garden of herself through the powers of the imagination. In the process, we have also moved closer to the narrative form of the parable.

Parabolic form is approached even more closely in "The Snake," the third of the stories on Woman under consideration. In it, the mystery of Woman is heightened by the fact that Steinbeck makes use of (but alters) an incident that took place in Ed Ricketts's lab to present supposedly objective observations in a supposedly objective milieu. The woman in this story has no name, however; she is neither Allen nor Teller. She is a case history: something that happened. She enters a scientist's domain with a special request—to purchase a snake and watch it feed. We learn nothing about her but her gender.

But in the process, she becomes a species watching another species—Woman watching reptile—and thereby she also becomes an intermediate subject for observation: she becomes Woman being watched by Man watching a reptile consume a rat. Man, the reader presumably included, is thus tempted to stand back and annotate the proceedings. In effect, she offers herself, albeit unintentionally, as datum.

Putting things another way, this is the third in a sequence of fictional relationships between men and women. Like Mary Teller's husband, Dr. Phillips recognizes through his experience with his woman visitor that he is lonely—"alone," as the story puts it. The same recognition would come to Doc in *Sweet Thursday*, but before what most readers take to be a sentimentalized, hence improbable, mating ritual. In the two laboratory stories, however, the objective scientist is made to discover his aloneness through contact with the other "species," Woman. Dr. Phillips is introduced as being methodical in his life and work, which are inseparable as routines from one another. He will stroke a cat moments before coolly putting it to death to become a science exhibit. The woman, when she arrives, is not interested in his preparation of slides; indeed, her presence causes him to abort a preparation sequence. The dispassionate technician is moved by the sight of the woman to want to "shock" her and reach her; in fact, the operative word is "arouse" (*TLV*, p. 77). Her apparent passivity is the motivation—something he thinks must signal a low metabolic rate, "almost as low as a frog's." As the story progresses, the woman's black, seemingly unfocused eyes seem to become "dusty," the word used to describe Jelka's in "The Murder" (pp. 77–78, 86).

Many have noted the empathy between woman and snake, something Steinbeck heightens for artistic purposes, partially by having Dr. Phillips be alone with the woman. No other male observers are present, which apparently was also the case in the real-life basis for the story; thus the woman's imitation of the snake's movements—which Steinbeck avoids having to make truly bizarre by having Phillips turn away while the snake devours the rat—takes on a semblance of the grotesque that it might not otherwise possess for anyone who has bottle-fed an infant and observed his or her own imitative response. Phillips had expected empathy for the rat, not the snake, but the woman has surprised him, and he feels almost a moral revulsion for what he has allowed to occur, for he objects to making sport of "natural processes." The killing of the snake is to the scientist "the most beautiful thing in the world," "the most terrible thing in the world"(*TLV*, p. 83). This is that "burning bright" force of life and death in the universe which Man may worship and measure; Woman simply embodies it naturally—as the Other.

It should be remembered that the woman specifically requests a *male* snake as her surrogate, a snake that, when it is about to devour its prey, almost seems to "kiss" the rat's body (TLV, pp. 78–79, 84). In "The Murder," communication between the genders is achieved in a way—through violence—but the three stories under discussion are united by sexual ambivalence, and repressed sexuality expresses itself through the male, the animal, and even the aggressor. As a scientist, Phillips is capable of criticizing this anecdote as literature, like Ethan Allen Hawley's self-conscious posturings as Jesus and Judas. But all he has read about what he calls "psychological sex symbols" does not help him understand the mystery of Woman. Clearly, this man who intended to shock and arouse has himself been sexually troubled—attracted and repulsed—by his visitor, whom he vows to leave to her practices "alone," but for whom he then searches the streets of his town for "months" afterward, never again encountering her (p. 86). "The Snake" is thus what the movies used to call a "different kind of love story."

It is notable that Steinbeck wrote these stories while he was married to his first wife, Carol, surely a remarkable woman even in a life rife with remarkable women. But my purposes are not those of biographical speculation. I am interested in the way in which, as these stories appear in *The Long Valley* one after another, the stage slowly turns 180 degrees until Man, not Woman, is downstage, and the audience has to look a distance upstage to see Woman through his eyes. In such extended works as *The Grapes of Wrath* and *The Wayward Bus* Steinbeck shows the spheres of activity of men and women as separate worlds with separate rituals, practices, and arcana. Yet Steinbeck, as I noted in my paper for the Tenth Salinas Steinbeck Festival in 1989,[10] regularly referred to his work in the writing of *Grapes* as "she" or "her." This is usage common to men who, like Juan Chicoy in *Bus*, work on the engines of automobiles and buses. But Steinbeck's text is as lubriciously female as any that might titillate and tantalize such a critic as the late Roland Barthes.[11] As I have also noted before, Steinbeck's muse was clearly a woman. Hence his artistry is a love affair of sorts, and if we wish to find the embodiment of the remarkable (if Other) Woman he knew in "real life," it is in his art that we must seek it, or her.

II

In *The Pastures of Heaven*, Steinbeck described an Edenic landscape that inspired the men who set eyes upon it with the vain ambition to impose their wills upon it. That this landscape is described in feminine terms is as evident there as it is in *The Long Valley*. The stories we have been looking at, with their two gardens and a snake, suggest that the locus of the discovery of the knowledge of good and evil is a feminized Edenic landscape, and that within that landscape men struggle to understand their destinies—destinies altered by the appearance of Woman in their midst. To strain the analogy just a bit more, it could be argued that moral struggle in Steinbeck's fiction is in a very real sense an Adamic attempt to tame—or *name*, and thus subdue—Woman, or womanly ambiguity. A recent student of mine has shown quite forcefully, for instance, that in that very moral and final Steinbeck novel *The Winter of Our Discontent*, Ethan Allen Hawley is saved by discovering, in his daughter, Ellen, the synthesis of the values represented by wife Mary and seductress Margie Young-Hunt.[12] In *East of Eden*, the moral quandary of Cathy Ames is "solved" by Abra, in an extension of the same sort of thinking. But this is to go even beyond the identification of Woman with setting, or even with plot. It is to argue the oneness of Woman and Steinbeck's art itself.

Within that oneness, however, exists a duality that may at first escape the reader's attention. In whatever manner these stories show Woman as Other, the fact that men do not understand them whether or not they seek to is not enough of a commonality to generalize further. The conventionalized lives of Elisa Allen and Mary Teller are in differing degrees the products of their own doing, expressed, as with the very different woman in "The Snake," as gender confusion. The latter woman expresses that confusion, however, not merely by means of emulation of the *male* but by imitation of the *animal* as well. It could be argued that many of Steinbeck's males are so domesticated that in a time more oriented to-ward strictly gender-determined role-playing, they—not the women—stood a great risk of being accused of being the repositories of normalcy, the ones someone like Huck Finn might have feared would "sivilize" him. I realize that I am putting a cosmetic face on a process of taming that others would prefer to blame on the women, but it is often the women in Steinbeck who *dare*, even when they fail to conquer when they stoop. They dare by straining against the traces they find themselves in, or, to put it biblically, they kick against the pricks—or their husbands. Some of them delve into animality to reach for a new stage of evolution. Consider Jelka from "The Murder"; include her and her husband's descriptions of her in animal terms, for example, and you just might have to accom-modate a woman whose intentions of getting her husband's attentions on her own terms could reach the extreme of bring-ing about the slaying of her cousin. Jelka's accommodation with her husband can be put on a level with that of "Jerry and the Dog" in Albee's *Zoo Story*, but it is also a leap beyond the norm of behavior that shocks and staggers us—like the ending of *The Grapes of Wrath* or *Burning Bright*.

In this sense, many of Steinbeck's women can be seen, if not as extraordinary individuals in the career sense, at least as what the jargon of another field of study might term "facilita-tors"—those who make it possible for others, especially men, to advance to new levels of comprehension, or community. When the men are reduced to drawing lines in the dirt, the women are seizing jackhammers—and baring their breasts to strangers. Two of my former students, Judy Wedeles and Beth Everest, have pointed to the surprising centrality of women in *East of Eden*, including—seemingly irrelevantly—by flying in the air.[13] The willingness to be gravid, but not bound by

gravity, seems another and perhaps fairer way of characterizing Steinbeck's women. To put things another way, though
these women often do not play by the rules, they manage to
achieve *autonomy*. They do so without bothering to consult
with the men, and, of course, that leaves the men mystified and
uncertain. It is in this sense that I suggest that Steinbeck's
approach to his art resembles the way he presents his women.
They are the art *and* the women, up to God-knows-what in the
powder room; they are Delphic and arcane and beyond control.
They are autonomous and will likely change on a man at any
moment. They are, in effect, *process*.

Men's work and women's work are often kept separate in
Steinbeck, most notably in *The Wayward Bus*. I am not suggesting the contrary, but something closer to the notion that
"man's work" *is* Woman. "She" is unpredictable and apt to
follow her own lead no matter what plans the man has made
for her. He may sharpen his pencils of a morning and write his
intentions in a journal to his editor, but that does not predict
that his work will obey his wishes; rather, he will obey *it*. In a
letter to Dennis Murphy edited and introduced by Robert
DeMott, Steinbeck wrote that "your only weapon is your
work."[14] But he also advised Murphy to keep his work "pure
and innocent and fierce." That is an interesting sequence of
adjectives, and one that might seem to make no sense in the
normal scheme of things. To some married men, however,
including Steinbeck, they might very well seem to be the
description of a wife.

In his introduction to the Murphy letter DeMott notes that
Steinbeck described his "words" as his "children," and surely
this notion is also worth pursuing critically. Certainly, the
Murphy letter does end by describing "creativeness" as "pre-
cious stuff" of which the world has very little. But if, without
stretching things too far, I can use this almost Whitmanesque

terminology to refer to the finished books as the author's seed, I can just as well refer to the creative act itself in sexual terms. The work is to be "pure and innocent and fierce," but the work is also one's "only weapon." Steinbeck was involved in his never-to-be-finished Arthurian project when he wrote to Murphy, and indeed, there is a palpable tone of knightly questing about the letter. I don't doubt, therefore, that when Steinbeck speaks of a "weapon" he is subconsciously thinking of a sword, and when and if he does, he is also introducing more sexual ambivalence into his imagination of a "female" body of writing. The results of this ambivalence are the same as they are in the short stories, for when the writer has performed well, Steinbeck tells Murphy, it is because he has been able to preserve his "holy loneliness." So the holiness of the love object transfers to the creator, but in the process he becomes isolated and aware of his incompleteness.

Interestingly, Ernest Hemingway was at work on what eventually was published as *The Garden of Eden* while Steinbeck was working on the Arthurian project and writing the letter to Murphy. That novel about sexual ambivalence may remind us of the Eden story in Genesis, where the acquisition of the knowledge of good and evil is customarily associated with the realization of sexual identity, after which the Garden is closed off to the honeymoon couple and guarded by an angel with a fiery sword. East of Eden, however, the human race goes on, and considerably more creatively. I spoke above of the husband-wife analogy between the writer as Steinbeck sees "him" and "his" work. Certainly Steinbeck was recovering from contentious marriages to two exceptional women when he wrote those lines, and it is not surprising that he would naturally think of a creative relationship as an adversarial one.

To Steinbeck, apparently, the art of fiction was tantamount

to a domestic argument. Somewhere along the line, the work was sure to develop a mind of its, or her, own, an appendage not at all in the cards in the beginning. Sooner or later it would want to "have its own head," something not unlike having its mind "coming out in the garden." The writer's capitulation to the autonomy of his own works is hardly unique, but his candor about the process may nearly be. In his tentative dedication of *East of Eden* to Pat Covici, Steinbeck refers to the period during which a writer is with his book as a time when they are "friends or bitter enemies but very close as only love and fighting can accomplish."[15] Early in the *Eden* journal, he developed the gender aspect of this notion at length:

> I do indeed seem to feel creative juices rushing toward an outlet as semen gathers from the four quarters of a man and fights its way into the vesicle. I hope something beautiful and true comes out—but this I know (and the likeness to coition still holds). . . . It seems to me that different organisms must have their separate ways of symbolizing, with sound or gesture, the creative joy—the flowering. . . . The joy thing in me has two outlets: one a fine charge of love toward the incredibly desirable body and sweetness of woman, and second— mostly both—the paper and pencil or pen.[16]

Moments later, his "mind blasted . . . with an idea so comely, like a girl, so very sweet and dear that I will put her aside for the book. Oh! she is lovely, this idea."[17] As said above, this way of relating to one's creative work is not unique to Steinbeck, though possibly the intensity described may be; indeed, the word "comely" here may remind us of the ardor expressed in the Song of Solomon, in which case it is only mildly far-fetched to say that for Steinbeck, the work *is* the Rose of Sharon.

Putting himself down on the left-hand pages of the *Eden* journal, Steinbeck then went on to set down on the right-hand sheets Woman, his work. The day's work done, the journal closed, the two lay together in the dark. My quest for Steinbeck's elusive Woman has not been meant to seem a glib response to Gladstein's salient questioning about the absence of remarkable women in Steinbeck's work. Rather, it suggests one means of answering her concerns by noting one way in which his work mirrors the life he lived, for if the twinned creative outlets for Steinbeck's "juices" were Woman and work, then ultimately Steinbeck's elusive and remarkable Woman is the work herself.

2

ROBERT DEMOTT

After *The Grapes of Wrath*

A Speculative Essay on John Steinbeck's Suite
of Love Poems for Gwyn, "The Girl of the Air"

for Susan Shillinglaw and Sue Ditsky

*He simply manufactured the woman he wanted, rather like that en-
lightened knight in the Welsh tale who made a wife entirely out of flowers.
Sometimes the building process went on for quite a long time, and when it
was completed everyone . . . was quite confused.*

—Steinbeck, "About Ed Ricketts" (1951)

I

Next to the tumultuous shapings and seizings of the romantic imagination—those magical and buoyant moments when
we fall in love, or when we enter the luminous presence of a
great fictive work (which is, I think, another kind of erotic
tantalization both for reader and writer)—there are few more

exciting events in the life of the literary scholar than the discovery of previously unknown writings by a favorite author, especially when they point to a dimension of that writer's life not revealed in the assembled archives and published records of his career. Obviously, there will always be lacunae to be filled in accounts of a writer's life. In John Steinbeck's case this is especially valid, for the past decade has been quite generous in turning up documents that illuminate otherwise shadowy areas of his life. I recall San Jose State University's acquisition of Steinbeck's correspondence to Wanda Van Brunt, the former Mrs. Mark Marvin, whose husband was one of the production managers of Steinbeck's film script, *The Forgotten Village* (1941). Written over eleven months, from September 1948 to August 1949, these thirty-one letters, purchased in October 1985 by San Jose's Steinbeck Research Center, add particulars to one of the bleakest eras of the novelist's life, when, reeling from personal setbacks, he retreated to his family's Eleventh Street house in Pacific Grove, California, to lick his wounds. These letters are all the more valuable because Van Brunt's name is not mentioned in Steinbeck biographies or letter publications, though she was one of several people responsible for his emotional rescue during his soul's dark night.[1]

If the mark of an important writer is the capacity to keep surprising us with wilderness areas, then I believe Steinbeck qualifies. Whenever we think we have safely arrived at a consensus about him, fresh evidence turns up that causes us to view his life and/or his career anew. But John Ditsky said it succinctly in his speech, "John Steinbeck—Yesterday, Today, and Tomorrow," which opened Steinbeck Festival IX in Salinas in 1988: "Once we have piled up enough data about the 'linear' [chronological] Steinbeck . . . we can begin the effort to see him

whole—whatever that may prove to mean for his future reputation."[2] As with all of Ditsky's insights—including his excellent keynote address for this Third International Steinbeck
Congress—I believe these are sound words we can all live by;
they echo my sentiments precisely. But first we need to possess
more of the facts, which is why I so strongly encourage inves-
tigation among Steinbeck's far-flung unpublished archives,
encouragement I hope the following circuitous excursion into
an uncharted area of Steinbeck's career will provide.

II

Several years ago, in that antediluvian age before Jackson J.
Benson's monumental biography of Steinbeck, I had just
turned in the manuscript of *Steinbeck's Reading* to Garland
Publishing Company (the book was published in 1984), and I
was beginning the earliest forays into editing a diary Steinbeck
kept during and after his writing of *The Grapes of Wrath*
(1939). The typed manuscript, housed at the Harry Ransom
Humanities Research Center at the University of Texas in
Austin, stretches intermittently from February 1938 through
January 1941. Through the palest, most muted of allusions
in one late entry, I intuited some clandestine activity by
Steinbeck, some subterfuge carried on without the knowledge of Carol Henning Steinbeck, his resourceful, talented,
straight-speaking wife of the 1930s, who had, perhaps more
than anyone else, facilitated Steinbeck's maturation from the
jejune literary style of the Don Byrnne-inspired *Cup of Gold*
(1929) to the unflinching critical temperament of *In Dubious
Battle* (1936), *Of Mice and Men* (1937), and *The Grapes of
Wrath*. (The latter, as if to underscore the irony of personal
history, is dedicated "To CAROL Who Willed It." Steinbeck's

veiled journal reference to "the other"—was it a person, or some secret writing?—intrigued me and piqued my gossip-mongering curiosity, especially when I eventually discovered that the unsuspected, embedded writing, the text beneath the text, so to speak, was a suite of love poems produced secretly for Gwendolyn Conger. After protracted machinations, Gwyn (I adopt her preferred spelling for the rest of my essay) would become Steinbeck's lover and, from 1943 to 1948, his second wife and mother of his only children. But before that, to protect their anonymity, they concocted elaborate smoke screens and cryptic communiqués, addressed through Max Wagner, their go-between in Hollywood. "Will you also tell the secretary," Steinbeck wrote Wagner in late 1940, "that the heat is on the mail a little bit and some other arrangements will have to be worked out. Fix that at the next meeting of the club."[3]

Meanwhile, Benson's biography appeared in late 1984. His indispensable account of the disastrous John/Carol/Gwyn relationship added much to the one-sided account in *Steinbeck: A Life in Letters* and filled in many gaps in my own emerging structure of the triangle. Benson's emphasis on Steinbeck's propensity to idealize Gwyn out of all proportion to her character coincided with my own intuitions in the matter.[4] But unless you read his book very closely, you might have missed two of the sources for his characterization: "Only by reading his love letters and the dozens of love poems addressed to her can one comprehend the extent of his adoration" (*TAJS*, p. 620). I had already examined the thick bundle of Steinbeck's love-torn and frequently sad letters to Gwyn at the Bancroft Library at the University of California, Berkeley (these are absent from *Steinbeck: A Life in Letters*), but it wasn't until much later that Benson informed me that he had only glanced at the poems (which were then still owned by a very-much-alive Gwyn) during one of his interviews with her in the early 1970s. So, until I quoted them selectively in "Aftermath," the final bridging commentary in my edition of Steinbeck's *Grapes of Wrath* journal, the poems had not been in general circulation, not even excerpted in previous biographies on Steinbeck.[5]

The twenty-five poems have never been published in a separate format, and the original manuscript is hand-written in a small pocket-size notebook. When Gwyn died in 1975, the booklet was purchased by Richard Schwartz, owner of Stage House II Book and Art Gallery in Boulder, Colorado (where Gwyn had been living). In turn, at the direction of John and Gwyn's children—brothers Thom Steinbeck and the late John Steinbeck IV—Schwartz sold it, as part of a large archive of Gwyn's holdings, to the Jenkins Rare Book Company of Austin, Texas. John Jenkins retained much of the archive but sold the poetry manuscript to Black Sun Books of New York City. From Black Sun Books it was purchased in 1979 for $16,500 by Edwin and Anne-Marie Schmitz, recognized Steinbeck aficionados, collectors, and owners of the Book Nest in Los Altos Hills, California. In 1981 the Schmitzes donated the notebook to the John Steinbeck Library in Salinas, with the provision that it be sealed. While their precaution put the holographic manuscript out of circulation, the tale doesn't end there.[6]

Enter Terry G. Halladay, former literature manager of Jenkins Rare Books, who knew a good thing when he saw it. Drawing on the Gwyn Steinbeck Collection in 1977 *before* it was broken up and sold, Halladay transcribed nearly a dozen seven-inch reel-to-reel audiotapes containing Gwyn Conger Steinbeck's memoirs. In 1979 Halladay used the archive to produce his now-valuable M.A. thesis, "The Closest Witness," which concludes with Halladay's complete transcription of Steinbeck's love poems to Gwyn.[7]

Written for Gwyn Conger, practically under the nose of Carol Steinbeck (which explains the concealable pocket-size notebook), the poems were generated out of the adulterous longing and nostalgic "ache" (Poem 4) of Steinbeck's wayward heart as a means of bridging the distance between the lonely Lancelot in Los Gatos and his Guinevere in Hollywood. In the tradition of medieval love lyrics, Poem 1 functions as an address to his beloved (Gwyn's name is nowhere mentioned in the suite) and as an invocation to the eternal woman, a fantastic and impossible-to-attain combination of goddess and muse. She is the imagined fulfillment of his longing for "home," a chord that reverberates like a struck lyre throughout the sequence:

> I will speak to you always young,
>   young, milk-skinned
> Smelling of a sweetness that has
>   no simile;
> Smell of warm, young, clean skin,
> Smell of the unknown house
> And a dear home.
> I will address you always
> Although your name change
> And your sister sit
> In the seat you made warm.
>   ("CW," p. 301)

With apologies to Steinbeck, I am going to call his collection "The Girl of the Air," a convenient working title that comes from the major image of the fifteenth poem of his suite, the longest and, in many ways, the most revealing of the lot. If Steinbeck scholars wish to find a source for his courtly propensity to idealize/idolize Gwyn and to create seemingly reductive portraits of women in his fiction, they need look no further than this startling confession of a vision that occurred in his sixteenth year:

> Once in an empty year
> I, working in a field, hoeing weeds
> With a sharp hoe that flashed
> In and out of the soft earth,
> Painted in the air a girl and kept
>   her there
> Floating beside me to look at
>   to wonder at
> As I worked in the hot sun.
> And she, made of air and mind,
>   became eternal
> And all girls since have shared her,
> Have been a little piece of her.
>   ("CW," p. 315)

His beloved, invested with the sustaining qualities of this visionary woman, "red haired and lovely / White breasted with hard lusting nipples" has "taken the place of the air girl / Who floated beside me." Furthermore, the fatalism of Steinbeck's attraction is linked so deeply to his aggressive imagination that he writes, "You cannot save yourself from being / The girl of the air" ("CW," pp. 316–17). In this acquisitive leap, in this reductive formulation, Steinbeck crossed the line into a potentially tragic realm. With such expectations, what forgiveness could follow?

III

The time seems right, then, to put some solid feet under "The Girl of the Air." I am guessing that, fifty years later, these poems still provide an occasion for stimulating our curiosity and bridging our distances—sufficient reason, though they cannot exactly be called "great" art, for sharing Steinbeck's erotic text. Gwyn was of that opinion, too: "They are love poems . . . but the world is being denied them and I think that is a shame. John had a poetical mind. I am not saying the poems are comparable to William Blake or John Donne or even James Joyce, but they are beautiful and poignant . . . . They are not personalized as such, and I believe strongly that the world should know that he wrote these things" ("CW," pp. 275-76).

As with many suites, or serial poems, these are not lyrically even or logically coherent, but they do adhere in voice and subject to an inner, alogical romantic urgency, a quality of emotional promise balanced with despair at the lovers' separation. Despite many flat, prosaic lines and naive notions of lovers' complaints, Steinbeck often achieves a chimeric presence where his words of love and his love of words conjoin. For instance, in Poem 5—as throughout this sequence— Steinbeck's subject is the woman as sexual presence as well as textual articulation (a point tellingly observed by John Ditsky in the preceding chapter):

> I said I would make a song for you
> And not a dirge, but a song of fullness
> And fulfillment.
> My body is angry for your lack
>   And there is a death in every night
> And little birth in the morning of loneliness.
> ("CW," p. 305)

Indeed, I can't conceive of a more fitting setting or moment to offer the following exploratory observations. The audience is distinguished, the occasion is special, the atmosphere is suitably celebratory. We are gathered this close to what once must have surely been Eden to bear witness to Steinbeck's ability to challenge and surprise us as scholars, writers, readers, and—perhaps most of all—as sentient human beings. I should warn you that my method requires your forgiveness ahead of time, however, for it approaches the condition of randomness, which is to say, my talk emulates Steinbeck's approach in his 1951 memoir, "About Ed Ricketts," an account, you will recall, "which goes seesawing back and forth chronologically and in every other way" in its attempt to build "a whole picture."[8]

Perhaps, then, in this privileged place, this luxurious paradise of the senses, this frontier of lush imaginings, we might almost believe all over again—as I am convinced Steinbeck did—that "being in love," with its lusty guises and star-crossed shapes, is the key to life, the efficacious spur that propels the heart from hiding, grants the courage to defy reason, tradition, and common sense, encourages lovers to create impossible expectations, and motivates people to turn their backs on the past, and in so doing to redefine themselves as individuals and artists. Such passionate, rebellious bonding is first and foremost an act of imagination. Amid unrealistic expectations and reductive beliefs, Steinbeck produced this testament of faith in Poem 23, which measures perhaps better than anything else the depth of his commitment to Gwyn and the lengths to which he would go to follow his illicit desire:

> Whatever path time may clear for me on the
>   mountain
> Know this—that it will bend and curve and
>   climb
> Because of you. And going back and forth

I shall take the curves you contrived—
When I have forgotten the anguish of clearing
Still the path will curve, and I will
   make
Such turnings as the path describes.
                ("CW," p. 325)

Again in Poem 24, where Steinbeck's words create a climactic eternal present, a sexually charged, mystical penetration of lover/writer and beloved/reader: "I will speak to you always/I will speak to you out of all mouths. . . . Even when you have forgotten" (p. 326).

Already, though, I have gotten carried away by the magic of this time and place, and I have to remind myself that this fabled Hawaiian island doesn't always symbolize bliss. (In fact, Carol came here for several weeks in early 1941 at the beginning of a long separation prior to her divorce from John. Steinbeck himself visited Honolulu only once, in 1966, on his way to report approvingly on President Lyndon B. Johnson's disastrous war in Vietnam.) So instead of perpetuating the wrong impression with my somewhat pretentious-sounding title and introduction, I will warn you that my essay might as easily have been called "Of Lust and Men," or "The Pheromones of Wrath," because in a very real sense what I speak of today is a prototypical human fable of chemical attraction, a Steinbeckian parable of the fall from innocent, tender bonding to bitter, violent denunciation. "If I were to think of it in astrological terms," Gwyn recalled, "John was a Pisces and I a Scorpio. Scorpios and Pisces make great lovers, but they don't stay married long" ("CW," p. 277).

It is an old drama—probably the oldest of all—but one the mystical, chivalric (and perhaps repressed) Steinbeck had never acted in before. Between a settled but romantically thin existence of domestic attachment and financial security with Carol, and an exciting life of uncertain future but passionate feeling with Gwyn, Steinbeck vacillated miserably in late 1940 and early 1941. "My nerves cracked to pieces and I told Carol the whole thing, told her how deeply involved I was and how little was left," he explained to agent Mavis McIntosh. "She said she wanted what was left and was going to fight. So there we are. All in the open, all above board. I'm staying with Carol as I must. I don't know what Gwyn will do nor does she. Just as badly tied there as ever—worse if anything. . . . Anyway, Carol won the outside and G the inside and I don't seem able to get put back together again" (*SLL*, p. 227). His head was in one place, his heart in another, until a few weeks after the confrontation between Carol and Gwyn at the Steinbecks' Eardley Street house in Pacific Grove in April 1941, when the victor finally walked off with the spoils. The rest, as they say, is history.

While this exercise in prurient biography is both a footnote to Benson's *The True Adventures of John Steinbeck, Writer* and an elaboration on the last section of my *Working Days*, it is perhaps most of all a cautionary tale. It originated in that other ironic Eden of California, but it can and does apply everywhere the human heart seeks the fulfillment it cannot or should not have. The only thing worse than not getting what you want, Oscar Wilde reminds us in *Lady Windemere's Fan*, is getting what you want. But here I am rushing ahead of myself and will only say now that, in his writings of the early 1950s, including *Burning Bright, East of Eden*, and *Sweet Thursday*, Steinbeck eventually found recompense—even revenge—for getting his heart broken.

IV

Nineteen thirty-nine was a watershed year for Steinbeck. I put it mildly when I say that it was an exceptionally difficult one. It had been a trying winter, physically speaking. He was laid up or impaired for weeks on end with dental problems, tonsillitis, and severe sciatica, part of it—along with sheer mental exhaustion—the ironic fruit of his sedentary vocation. For five months the previous year—from late May through late October 1938—Steinbeck hunched daily over the outsized ledger book at the desk of his tiny, cramped workroom in his Greenwood Lane house in Los Gatos, where he parceled out his two-thousand-word allotment on what would become— though he wasn't then convinced—his most magnificent achievement, *The Grapes of Wrath*. Here, for example, is a representative journal entry, number 97, for October 20, 1938: "A late start. After last night it is no wonder. My nerves blew out like a fuse and today I feel weak and powerless. I wish it hadn't happened until I was through. Guess I better not press my luck. Just write today until I am tired and not force it. . . . I hope the close isn't controlled by my weariness" (*WD*, p. 91).

A tired, harried man, stressed all the time by a thousand demands on his time and attention, Steinbeck finished *The Grapes of Wrath* in a depleted, entropic state, a fragile psychic condition like advanced aging, or spiritual death. The cumulative strain of physical impairment and mental exhaustion took an enormous toll in the late fall of that year and the winter of the next.

But in some ways, the spring and summer of 1939 were even worse. With the incredible success of *The Grapes of Wrath* (published officially on April 14, 1939), Steinbeck got what he thought he wanted, though when success as a novelist arrived full-blown at his doorstep, it shook him so deeply that he needed to run from it, escaping, if at all possible, into anonymity. First he fled to Chicago, where he interned with Pare Lorentz, who was filming *The Fight for Life*. Later he was in and out of Hollywood, where ostensibly he consulted on the film scripts of *Of Mice and Men* and *The Grapes of Wrath*, but where, in June 1939, he met Gwyn Conger, a beautiful, twenty-year-old singer and aspiring actress who was then working in the chorus line at CBS Studios and doing bit-part work in an Irene Dunne movie, *Theodora Goes Wild*.

That fall—with Carol along—he took an automobile trip north to Seattle and to Vancouver, British Columbia, to visit musician John Cage and his wife, Xenia. (Steinbeck planned to write some musical pieces with Cage, though he apparently never followed up on them.) The following spring—again with Carol in tow—he sailed aboard the *Western Flyer* for a collecting trip with Ed Ricketts that would result in the collaborative book of travel and research, *Sea of Cortez*. Finally, he went back and forth to Mexico several times in 1940 and 1941 during the making of his film *The Forgotten Village*, directed by Herbert Kline.

During some of these sojourns, particularly to Hollywood, Carol was left at their new home, a fairly isolated mountaintop ranch on Brush Road in Los Gatos. It fell on her shoulders to answer mail (sometimes 50 to 75 letters a day) and requests from strangers wanting their copies of *The Grapes of Wrath* signed, to fend off an incessant stream of uninvited telephone callers and visitors, to manage their increasingly complex financial arrangements with agents McIntosh and Elizabeth Otis, and otherwise to keep a lid on an explosive situation, not an easy task for a person who was herself volatile, independent, moody, and restless, and who considered herself deserving of more honorable treatment.

The steady, unrelenting sale of *Grapes* between March and December of 1939 brought unprecedented fame, notoriety, and financial success to the Steinbecks, exceeding their wildest dreams. But it also tested their collective resistance and brought personal chaos, domestic discord, and intense unhappiness to husband and wife, whose marriage had already been cracking under earlier strains. "Something has to be worked out or I am finished writing," the novelist complained to Otis on June 22, 1939. "I went south to work and I came back to find Carol just about hysterical. She had just been pushed beyond endurance" (*SLL*, p. 185). Carol, Steinbeck told Otis a month later, is "pretty shell shocked too. . . . My nerves are just about worn out. . . . My leg is still painful but gradually receding. . . . Amazing how it shot my nerves though. Several times I've felt as if I were going over the edge."[9] In mid-October, roughly a year after he had finished writing *The Grapes of Wrath*, while still wrestling with his paralysis and gauging the nearness of the precipice, Steinbeck was also entertaining the need to alter the direction of his life. Here is a revealing entry from *Working Days*, written on October 16, 1939, which is both a summary and a prophecy. Note especially the blight already tainting the rose of success:

It is one year less ten days that I finished the first draft of the *Grapes*. Then we came up here to the ranch and then my leg went bad and I had ten months of monstrous pain. . . . This is a year without writing (except for little jobs—mechanical fixings). The longest time I've been in many years without writing. The time has come now for orientation. What has happened and what it had done to me. In the first place the

Grapes got really out of hand, became a public hysteria and I
became a public domain. I've fought that consistently but I
don't know how successfully. Second, we are rich as riches
go. We have money enough to keep us for many years. We
have this pleasant ranch which is everything one could desire.
It lacks only the ocean to be perfect. We have comfort and
beauty around us and these things I never expected. Couldn't
possibly have expected. . . . Now I am battered with uncertainties. That part of my life that made the *Grapes* is over. . . .
I have to go to new sources and find new roots. . . . I don't
know whether there is anything left of me. I know that some
of my forces are gone. . . . My will to death is strengthened. In
a sense, my work is done because there wasn't much to me
in the beginning. But my mind ranges and ranges and
searches. . . . I must work alone. That is necessary. I must
think alone.

(*WD*, pp. 105–7)

If it changed forever the literary landscape of the United
States, *The Grapes of Wrath* altered Steinbeck just as drastically, because it made him vulnerable to sweeping internal
changes. Many "have speculated," biographer Benson writes
with his characteristic lucidity, "about what happened to
change Steinbeck after *The Grapes of Wrath*. One answer is
that what happened was the writing of the novel itself"(*TAJS*,
p. 392). Here, perhaps, is a private irony to parallel the tragic
aspects of his fiction: an isolated individual writer composed a
novel that extolled the virtues of a social group's capacity for
survival in a hostile world, but he was himself so "tractored"
under in the process that his vision of familial, interpersonal
bonding and those unique qualities—the angle of vision, the
vital signature, the moral indignation—that made his art ex-
emplary in the first place could never be repeated with the

same integrated force. Nor did Steinbeck really want to repeat himself. As he told Carlton Sheffield on November 13, 1939, "I must make a new start. I've worked the novel . . . as far as I can take it. I never did think much of it—a clumsy vehicle at best. And I don't know the form of the new but I know there is a new thing which will be adequate and shaped by the new thinking. Anyway, there is a picture of my confusion. How's yours?" (*SLL*, p. 194).

Amid the confusion, Steinbeck was clear about two things. He was sick of being constrained; what he wanted above all else, he told Sheffield, were "freedom from respectability" and "freedom from the necessity of being consistent" (*SLL*, p. 193). Fed up with the prison of his career, and already emotionally captivated by Gwyn, Steinbeck's life became a vicious circle: the more celebrated he became, the more resentful he turned toward Carol, whose brittle efficiency, managerial brusqueness, and violent mood swings only depressed him further. Suddenly, everything associated with his public fame and private success—especially his marriage—had become a repugnant "nightmare" to him. In withdrawing from Carol, Steinbeck threw himself into a variety of writing projects, hoping to resurrect the discipline necessary to become productive again, even though several of his new jobs were collaborations, a situation he never fully liked. He resolutely turned his back on the "clumsy" novel (between 1939 and 1945 he published eight books, only half of them fiction). Instead, he tried his hand at a whole new range of genres, including comic drama, documentary film, scientific prose, travel writing, and poetry. Especially with his love poems and with *Sea of Cortez*, Steinbeck traded his role as social documentarian for private expressionist.

As part of his complete revolution Steinbeck deliberately

cast off the straitjacket of novelist and took up the dashing coat of the man of letters. "Do you realize that the thing which seemed to be happening is happening," he lamented to Otis on April 21, 1940. "I'm so busy being a writer that I have not time to write anything" (*LTE*, p. 25). Ultimately, his new garment proved to be an imperfect fit, I think, but the experimental writing of this period—from late 1939 through 1942—situated him at the threshold of a new consciousness, an arena of endeavor that he believed more truly honored his own sense of liberated sexual and emotional transformation. After 1940 his writing centered on sustained explorations of new subjective topics—the dimensions of individual choice, romantic/domestic relationships, and imaginative consciousness—all of them with enormous potential for sentimentality, partial portraiture, and softened treatment. (To understand Steinbeck's willingness to resurrect a temperament he felt he had abdicated during his career with Carol, future scholars might have to consider the changes in Steinbeck's psychological and emotional makeup rather than in such causes as his alleged decline in artistic ability or his move from native California to adopted New York.)

So, on that fateful night in June 1939, Steinbeck—physically ill, crippled from sciatica, severely depressed, drinking too much for his own good while he hid out from publicity at the Aloha Arms Apartments off Hollywood's Sunset Boulevard—was visited by a stunning, red-haired showgirl. When Gwyn, a self-confessed "half-assed Florence Nightingale," brought him, at his friend Max Wagner's instigation, homemade chicken soup (which he hated) and tender ministrations (which he loved), the pheromones began to fly, a door opened in Steinbeck's heart, and he took the first step through. When he did, a whole structure of pastness began to crumble, and a new future rose like a bright promise to take its place. The poems themselves, like the condition of "home" they long to create, became the proof and the test of his knightly devotion; when his long-distance courting began, the text became a meeting point for reality and imagination, present and future, despair and desire, as in Poem 3:

> We will sit down together, my love,
> Red haired and lonely.
> And for a little while the winds
> Will go around. And the house chinks
> Will be tight: I will feel safe and warm
> In your strong weakness and you
>   in my weak strength,
> I will be young in your youth, and you
> Thinking I have seen future,
> Will feel a future more secure
> Against the winds.
> We will be wrong, my love, both wrong
> But our wrongness will be right and I
> Truly will be young who has never
>   been young;
> And you secure who are balanced
> In uncertainty.
>   ("CW," p. 303)

From the first, Steinbeck was slain by Gwyn. Like Petrarch, "Love caught him naked with his shaft." Much as Charles Smithson, the hero of John Fowles's *The French Lieutenant's Woman*, who, when he saw the mysterious, fascinating Sarah Woodruff for the first time, was lost forever, so Steinbeck was lost. By "lost," of course, I mean that immediate intuitive awareness that a large part of his earlier life—his professional respectability and station, his ten-year marriage to Carol based on discipline, sacrifice, and commitment, his sense of home and being in the world, perhaps even his sense of himself as a dutiful son—was instantly revealed to be false, or at least wanting in the kind of passionate emotion and potential for sexual fulfillment he had spent his whole life seeking in the hidden, perhaps traitorous, recesses of his heart. "I get so dreadfully homesick I can't stand it and then realize that it's not for any home I ever had," he confessed to Webster Street in December 1940 (*SLL*, p. 218).

It took Steinbeck four years to walk all the way over the threshold (after two years of separation, Carol and John divorced on March 18, 1943; eleven days later he married Gwyn) (*SLL*, p. 251; *TAJS*, p. 515), but once through he emerged a different man and, I think, a more experimental kind of writer. "What happened between us that night was pure chemistry," Gwyn later recalled in her autobiography ("CW," p. 36). Steinbeck agreed; in Poem 7, he wrote:

> Some where in the long seeking
> There has been a finding, a chemistry
> Out of two combinations of elements. . . .
> Atom finding orbit with atom
> Chest close fit with breast
> Lingham in yoni. . . .
>   the rarity of such chemistries. . . .
> The glory of synchronization of
>   ductless glands.
>   ("*CW*," p. 307)

That last line surely is one of the most horrid ever penned, but keep it in mind because I'll return to it later.

During the next eighteen months the relationship proceeded on again, off again; Steinbeck was deeply hooked, investing nearly everything in his imaginative creation of Gwyn that he felt was lacking in his own wife. In Poem 10, he wrote:

> This thing is good, to be taken and loved
> Although it crisp and die in our hands
> This thing is good although it wound us
> You and I—I who created you
> You who created me.
>
> ("CW," p. 310)

Even with this avowed, ironically prophetic risk of failure (a refrain in the suite), such desire was a shaky, ethereal foundation on which to construct a new life; such deep nostalgia for a shared, but unspecified, emotional "home" I think all of us gathered here today have probably experienced ourselves, just as we all probably come to realize such habitations exist mostly in the penumbra of longing. On the other hand, nothing ventured, nothing gained. In other words, if Richard Wilbur's catchy line, "love calls us to the things of the world," is true, then Steinbeck had no choice but to follow his bliss. He could not refuse the siren call because it must have seemed his destiny, an incomparable gift he had been waiting for all his life, a breakthrough with its own set of demands, requiring new codes of behavior and a new language to replace the old conventions. Compared to the "mannish" Carol, Gwyn was "all woman, every bit woman," Steinbeck crowed to McIntosh (*WD*, p. 99). But then, he had no idea what he was really in for, a point McIntosh understood quite well when she later complained he had "very peculiar ideas of women" in those days.[10]

V

When the majority of Steinbeck's readers, including the

most seasoned and knowledgeable students of his work, think of the dimensions of his literary career, they invariably base their assessment on his achievements in three genres: his novels and short fiction, his dramas and screenplays, and his nonfiction prose. In this summary of familiar modes, poetry is conspicuously absent. My guess is that Steinbeck is rarely thought of as a poet outside of some notable elevated passages in his fiction: the emotionally engaged, densely symbolic, nakedly dithyrambic intercalary sections of *The Grapes of Wrath* or, in a more muted vein, the sure, quiet lyrical touches of "The Chrysanthemums" and *The Red Pony*. Furthermore, even for the informed follower of his career, Steinbeck is considered a poet (better yet a "versifier") only in connection with his college juvenalia, his occasional bawdy verses, such as the "Ballad of Quid Pro Quo" and others (excerpted by Carlton A. Sheffield in his introduction to *Letters to Elizabeth*), or the controversial homoerotic poems by "Amnesia Glasscock," still frequently and erroneously attributed to Steinbeck, though in fact they were written by Carol.

And yet from William Herbert Carruth's class on versification (English 35) at Stanford University, which Steinbeck took in spring 1923 (one of only six A's he received in college), through the late stages of his career, Steinbeck not only read a great deal of poetry but also did in fact write it. Not all his poems have been preserved, because for him—and this is an important qualification—poetry was a type of private utterance, a kind of personal exercise akin to his journal keeping, and meant, as he once said of Robinson Jeffers's intentions, to "exorcise" demons from the household. Steinbeck seems to have indulged in poetry for various reasons, including his plain and simple love of words, as therapy when he was temporarily blocked in his attempts to write a book, and, in the present case, his desire to express and validate passionate personal feelings, such as "the ache of loneliness" and the mystical belief that a woman's love, like a sacred grail, brings the quester salvation found nowhere else. In critic Mimi Reisel Gladstein's terms, Gwyn becomes yet another avatar of the "indestructible woman," prominent in so much of his fiction.[11] In Poem 20, Steinbeck writes, "If this venomous race survive/ You and your symbol only can save it" ("CW," p. 322), lines that reach back to Ma Joad and Rose of Sharon in *The Grapes of Wrath* and forward to Juana, Mordeen, Abra Bacon, and Suzy in *The Pearl* (1947), *Burning Bright* (1950), *East of Eden* (1952), and *Sweet Thursday* (1954), respectively.

"Please tell Gwyn that I am making a song for her and I have never made a song for anyone else," Steinbeck informed his confidant Max Wagner on November 23, 1940. "I love you both. And protect her a little, please. For she is dear to me" (*SLL*, p. 217). This external reference to the poems' composition, plus some internal ones from the songs themselves—"I said I would make a song for you" (Poem 5, which I quoted earlier), "red leaves under the mountain frost" (Poem 6, which accurately describes autumn conditions in the Santa Cruz Mountains), "the colored bird who is life and death" (Poem 9, which describes the totemic, mummified birds, each in its own wooden coffin, that Steinbeck picked up from a medicine woman in Mexico earlier in the year)—help locate the poems in time and place. They also identify the oblique references to "the other" as Steinbeck's code word both for Gwyn and for the suite of poems he was writing for her right under Carol's otherwise watchful eye. Further, they help explain the frequent tone of paranoia and arcane allusion in his entries in the post-*Grapes of Wrath* section of *Working Days* and in *Steinbeck: A Life in Letters*, though once we realize he is alluding to Gwyn in Hollywood, his subterfuge becomes clear. He wrote the suite of poems for Gwyn at his Biddle Ranch home in Los Gatos between late September and late November 1940, between trips back and forth to Mexico and Hollywood for the filming and editing of *The Forgotten Village*. Here was Steinbeck talking to himself in entry 119, written on December 12, 1940; once again, note the prophetic tone, the need to whistle in the dark: "Back from Mexico again and this time I'm through there I hope. And back from Hollywood again and definitely not through there. I try to stay relaxed about that. It isn't possible to be more than it is, and I know that. What a fiasco that would be. And I like it and will continue. It seems the best thing to do and surely the pleasantest in many ways, but there are stomach pains in it too. How will it end— tragically, I imagine, but that is part of it too. I won't even run from that" (*WD*, p. 122).

In the manner of two of Steinbeck's favorite models— Synge's translation of Petrarch's *Sonnets to Laura* and Mathers's translation of *Black Marigolds*—both of which were capable of moving him to tears, these poems also have a fragile sadness, a transcendent, almost mystical strain, and a resonance of lament that haunts the whole suite. But Gwyn was not the angelic Laura, unapproachable and chaste, so the thrust of these poems also testifies to the power of human sexuality, mutual intimacy, physical attraction, and—perhaps above all else—the dignity of lovemaking.

In the late 1930s John and Carol's relationship was often celibate. If the cryptic entries in *Working Days* and Gwyn's recollections of her candid confrontation with Carol in "The Closest Witness" can be believed, Steinbeck did not mix intercourse and writing during his marriage; apparently, he and Carol occupied separate beds, both at the Greenwood Lane house and later at the Biddle Ranch.[12] Beginning in 1938, their separateness probably had become habitual, and while this is salacious conjecture on my part, it does help explain that when Steinbeck made love to Gwyn the first time (according to Gwyn's memoir, this took place in Oceanside in the summer of 1940), "the glory of synchronization of ductless glands" quickly obliterated most traces of his marital faithfulness and reason. The explicit recollection of sexual pleasure and the praise of Gwyn's physical attributes, especially her hair, symbol of her universal power, comprise a holy spell, a magic incantation—"Oh! Red and gold and black"—that, the blissful lover concludes, "has been God in many times to many men./ And still is God" (Poem 8; "CW," p. 308).

As Steinbeck later confided to Mavis McIntosh, Gwyn's "affectionate" presence transformed his entire life and made his "indulgences" (the risk that his work would "suffer") seem worthwhile. "The house is easy and it has been so long since I have lived in an easy house. My work has jumped in amount and I don't have to fight it. My sex life is prodigious and I take strength rather than depletion from it."[13] Is it any wonder, then, that Carol failed to regain her husband? Against Steinbeck's holy distortion and Gwyn's fleshly magic she didn't have a mortal's chance of success. If Carol's side of the story has been a long time coming to light, at least she can be credited with the most realistic assessment of her husband's behavior and subsequent actions. "He left me for a better piece of ass," she is reported to have said in 1948.[14]

VI

If 1939 was a trying year for Steinbeck, 1948 was a tragedy. His two soul mates left him—in May, Ed Ricketts was killed in an auto/train crash; in August, Gwyn told him she wanted a divorce. The combined force of these two blows nearly destroyed Steinbeck. The gruesome story of his bitter crash and demoralization, his violent moods and fierce, uncompromising misogyny, and his sense of betrayal and rejection, as well as the slow struggle toward recovery with Elaine, is told in Benson's biography and in his more recent *Looking for Steinbeck's Ghost* (Norman: University of Oklahoma Press, 1988), as well as in the many letters from that period printed in *Steinbeck: A Life in Letters*, in Thomas Fensch's *Steinbeck and Covici: The Story of a Friendship* (Middlebury, Vt.: Paul S. Eriksson, 1979), and in Steinbeck's correspondence with Wanda Van Brunt.

Steinbeck's obsessive urge to make a goddess of Gwyn, then accuse her of being a monster when she failed to live up to his impossible standards, does not automatically absolve Gwyn of her share of provocation and blame (she later called their marriage "tragic"), but it does suggest that his affair with her was the most intense romantic relationship he ever had. Though it wounded everyone involved, there is no denying that it remained a constant touchstone of his personal and literary experience for more than a decade. Steinbeck was fond of repeating the story of how Ed Ricketts, very much like Lleu Llaw Gyffes, "that enlightened knight in the Welsh tale" of *The Mabinogian*, "manufactured" the woman he wanted. But the fact was that like Math, who conjured a woman "entirely out of flowers" for Lleu in the medieval epic, and like Ricketts, Steinbeck "built his own woman . . . created her from the ground up" (*Log*, p. li). Through another imaginative, linguistic investiture that compensated for his real-life experience, Steinbeck reprised his tumultuous marriage to Gwyn in the pathetic *Burning Bright* and went a long way toward exorcising his memory of her in his devastating portrait of the evil, conscienceless Cathy Ames in *East of Eden*. But it wasn't really until his next book, the slapdash comedy *Sweet Thursday*, that one of his characters—ironically, or perhaps fittingly, a woman—struck the summary note on the subject of Girls of the Air: "When a man falls in love it's ninety to one he falls for the dame that's worst for him." With that intentionally humorous, self-deprecating remark, Steinbeck brought to a close a bittersweet chapter in his emotional life that began fifteen years earlier.

3

ABBY H. P. WERLOCK

Looking at Lisa

The Function of the Feminine in
Steinbeck's *In Dubious Battle*

"It is terrible. But I hope when you finish it, in the
disorder you will feel a terrible kind of order."

So said John Steinbeck in a letter to his agent, Mavis McIntosh, in 1935, when he had finished *In Dubious Battle*.[1] Almost from the moment of the novel's publication in 1936, critics rose to the author's challenge, praising various forms of "order" in its realistic, moral, mythical, biblical, Miltonic, and Arthurian themes.[2] Steinbeck's art is unquestionably impressive here; like such contemporaries as T. S. Eliot and William Faulkner, he subtly blends mythical allusions so that the novel rises above mere allegory. Nor was this the first time he had written on such a scale. Pointing out Steinbeck's debt to Malory, Shakespeare, and Milton, Jackson J. Benson and Anne Loftis note that he had already created "characters of mythic dimension" in his 1933 novel *To a God Unknown*.[3] However, these mythical characters seem only to be male. Whereas

critics of *In Dubious Battle* see Mac, the party leader, Jim
Nolan, his young disciple, and Doc Burton, the philosophical
loner, as variations of the biblical Christ, the mythical
Prometheus, Milton's Satan, or Malory's Percival, these same
critics virtually ignore the novel's women—Jim's friend Lisa,
his mother Mrs. Nolan, and his sister May.

More than thirty years ago Peter Lisca pointed out that
Steinbeck's women are "overshadowed" by the more visible
men,[4] and perhaps for this reason we have failed to look at Lisa
and to fathom her meaning. Clearly, a complete understanding
of the novel requires attention to the women significant to Jim
Nolan, Lisa in particular. Moreover, the way Mac, Jim, and Doc
view and respond to Lisa determines each man's humanity. A
careful examination of the function of the feminine illuminates Steinbeck's juxtaposition of the dominant power of the
men to the quieter power of the women.

The research of Benson and Loftis into the labor camps of
the 1930s is invaluable in establishing the background of the
novel and in detailing Steinbeck's familiarity with migrant
workers, labor camps, strikes, and their leaders. Most significant is their finding that, despite remarkable similarities between the real and the fictional, Steinbeck took artistic liber-
ties with actual occurrences and people.[5] Thus Mimi Reisel
Gladstein argues convincingly that because of "the way Steinbeck readjusted his fictional world to omit the women who
populated his real world, the significance of those women he
wished to portray is intensified."[6]

Three of Steinbeck's "readjustments" of fact are particularly germane to the role of the women in *In Dubious Battle*.
First, a number of active strikers were women. According to
Benson and Loftis, they "often acted as 'guerilla picketers,'
circling around the police, who were confronting the male

strikers." Benson and Loftis cite one incident in which female picketers ran into the fields and cried out to the pickers, "Come on out, quit work; we'll feed you. If you don't, we'll poison all of you."[7] Second, a funeral was held for two workers, a man and a woman, shot and killed in a riot.[8] Third, Steinbeck knew in detail the characters and activities of Communist party members Pat Chambers and the fiery, eloquent, and fanatic young woman Caroline Decker, and almost certainly based the characters of Mac and Jim, respectively, on them.[9]

Thus the questions pertinent to understanding the role of women in *In Dubious Battle* are these: Why, knowing the visible role played by women in actual strikes, did Steinbeck eliminate the women from his extended fictional portraits of the pickers and strikers? Why, in his literary version of the funeral of the two strikers who had been shot to death, did he omit the fact that in reality one of the dead was a woman? And, perhaps most importantly, why did he turn the disciplelike figure of the young Communist party woman Caroline Decker into Jim Nolan? The answer may well lie in the reason Benson and Loftis suggest for his ignoring the ethnic mix of the California migrant workers: Steinbeck used only white characters in his novel because he did not wish to complicate his theme.[10] Although the same deduction could apply to his ignoring of these women, I suggest an additional reason: Steinbeck was using the image of woman in his novel to underscore and amplify mythical allusions and perhaps even to subvert some of them. It would therefore have been inappropriate to include women among the plotting, violent, and fanatic men. The novel certainly contains no Eves or Guineveres, for Lisa displays a shrewdness and moral restraint lacking in both these mythical predecessors.

Benson has noted that when Steinbeck wrote *To a God*

Unknown, he was influenced not only by the Bible and Frazer's *The Golden Bough*, but also by his reading of Robert Briffault's 1927 anthropological work *The Mothers*.[11] Moreover, according to Carol Steinbeck, *The Grapes of Wrath* (1939) was "pure Briffault."[12] Not surprisingly, then, *In Dubious Battle*, written between these two novels, is underpinned and framed by women or concepts of the feminine. Warren Motley tells us that Steinbeck, reading *The Mothers*, was influenced by Briffault's conviction that matriarchy, far from being an Amazonian sort of patriarchy, emphasizes a relationship between people based on cooperation rather than power.[13] In Briffault's words, "Women are the repositories of those [humane] values, and it is upon the rude foundations which they laid that the restless energy of man has reared a mighty structure of achievement."[14] Briffault concludes with a reference to *Faust* in which Goethe alludes "in mystic terms to the mothers that dwell beyond space and time, and from whom the manifestations of life proceed."[15] Steinbeck invokes these mystic mothers in two women, Lisa and Mrs. Nolan. Further, Steinbeck knew Joseph Campbell during this period, and Campbell has since observed that some of the mythical imagery in *In Dubious Battle*, particularly that of the Madonna, may have resulted from their discussions.[16] Therefore, the women of *In Dubious Battle* may be viewed as inheritors of female powers, not only in anthropological terms but in mythical terms as well.

Within the first few pages of the novel, as Jim speaks of feeling "dead," he tells a stranger, the Communist party man Harry Nilson, his family history. Both his parents are deceased, and his father, Roy Nolan, was well known for his violent propensities, which eventually resulted in his death—from a charge of buckshot in the chest—during an arson attempt. Jim seems to have inherited his anger and his temper from his father, but as Mac points out, Jim's old man knew only how to "fight": "I don't know where you learned to use your bean and keep clear," he says, and Jim replies that his intelligence and ability to reason derive from his mother.[17]

Although Mrs. Nolan is given no name, she acquires stature, not only because Jim continually recalls her, but also because she is the only character in the novel who professes any religious beliefs—and Jim seems to have inherited her spiritual tendencies as well. Memories of his mother frame the novel. At the beginning he tells Nilson that his mother was a Catholic, but his "old man wouldn't let her go to church. He hated churches" (*IDB*, p. 5). Only at the end, with the growing friendship of Jim and Lisa, do we comprehend the full force of the feminine in his life. Just before his own death Jim tells the rest of the story: sometimes his mother would take him to church in the middle of the week—even though his father would have been furious had he known of these religious pilgrimages—and Jim felt peaceful when looking at the statue of Mary the Mother.

Jim never seems to mourn his father's death, but he speaks of his mother's several times. Notably, he joins the Communist party, not after his father's death, but almost immediately after his mother's; part of his spirit seems to have departed with her. At her death he has lost both women in his life, and he tells their stories. When he was still a boy, his older sister, May, suddenly vanished one day. She was fourteen, a pretty girl with yellow hair. Despite police questionings of her schoolgirl friends, the mystery of her disappearance remains unsolved, but the clear implication is that she was abducted. From that point on his mother, whose light-blue eyes become like "white stones," with "a kind of dead look," is miserable, voiceless, silenced, "quieter even than before" (*IDB*, pp. 9–10).

The implied allusion here may well be to the goddess Demeter who, robbed of her beloved daughter, Persephone, is utterly grief-stricken. Indeed, the well-known fourth century B.C. statue of Demeter depicts a motionless, stone-eyed, mourning mother. Frazer sees Demeter and Persephone as human embodiments of corn and symbols of rebirth,[18] and thus May's yellow hair allies her with the corn goddess. Persephone was picking flowers with friends when she was abducted to Hades and raped by the god of the underworld, and May was apparently sitting on the steps talking and giggling with her girlfriends when she vanished. A common interpretation of the myth is that Demeter and Persephone, mother and daughter, together represent the timeless, enduring quality of the feminine, extending backward and forward in time; their union was central to the ritual performed in the Eleusinian mysteries. Gladstein quotes C. Kerenyi's view that "Persephone is, above all, her mother's Kore; without her, Demeter would not be *Meter*."[19] Moreover, along with Hecate, the moon goddess, mother and daughter constitute the "tripartite woman," as do Persephone and her friends, Artemis and Athena: Persephone, passively unaware when raped, represents the sexual side of woman; Artemis, the huntress, represents the active, assertive side; and Athena, goddess of wisdom, the intellectual and spiritual side. Together, as Gladstein notes, they form the "triune Kore."[20]

Demeter is much more assertive than Persephone, but Persephone is the symbol of spring and renewal.[21] They complement each other and after Persephone's abduction Demeter manages to reunite with Persephone for eight months of every year, plunging the earth into barren darkness during the other four months as she awaits her daughter's return. Similarly, as her name suggests, May, disappearing to some sort of netherworld, signifies the disappearance of spring and life from her mother's world. But Mrs. Nolan, denied the happier ending of the Demeter story, becomes a study in tragedy: forbidden to practice her faith, to worship, she is literally silenced by a perpetually blood-soaked, violent husband whom she must cleanse after each of his fights. Inevitably, when robbed of her beloved daughter, Mrs. Nolan—her own life become a dark underworld—no longer cares whether she lives or dies. Her fate rendering her powerless, Mrs. Nolan suggests Persephone as well as Demeter. Jim recalls that on her deathbed she was speechless, not even responding when he asked if she would like to see a priest: "She didn't answer me, just stared. . . . I guess she just didn't want to live. I guess she didn't care if she went to hell, either" (*IDB*, p. 5). Not until the end of the novel, moments before his death, does Jim explain her significance in his life and simultaneously reiterate her silence: "She wouldn't speak to me, she just looked at me. She was hurt so bad she didn't even want a priest. I guess I got something burned out of me that night" (p. 242).

Jim thus loses his father, his youthful sister, May, and his mother who, like Athena, has imparted to him wisdom and spirit. However, only after losing his mother, source of his spiritual values, does he describe himself as "dead"; attempting a rebirth through the Communist party, he heads to the East. Curiously, he tries to distance himself from women who, like his past, seem connected both with his own death and with that of his mother and sister. In the past, women were objects in brothels to whom he would go when he became "riled up" (*IDB*, p. 27). Now he neither drinks nor smokes nor goes with women.

As he joyously hops the freight train, apprenticed to Mac on his first assignment, Jim seems very much a Percival figure, as Warren French has noted.[22] He is certainly on a quest, a journey, as he travels away from the city he equates with his death. Like Percival with a vision of the grail, or Adam when looking at Eden before the Fall, Jim sits in the open doorway of the train, watching the farms go by with their "big market vegetable gardens" and "great white dairy barns" (*IDB*, p. 28). However, although the beckoning potential of the apple trees hangs heavily over the story throughout the novel, Jim's vision of fruitful farms is undercut by the dark masculine realities of deceit, violence, and death. At this point the train ride's pastoral, Edenic views give way to black nightmares, and their destination is repeatedly described as a "jungle" (p. 33, 40, 89).

As Jim continues his initiation into the darkness, the jungle, and the Communist party, the ritual occasions the entrance of a third woman into his life: when they arrive at the camp the darkness is broken by three white tents, "and in one of them a light burned and huge black figures moved on the canvas" (*IDB*, p. 35). Suggesting a religious oil painting on canvas, the scene is imbued with a mystical quality. Lisa, wife of Joey London, son of London the strike organizer, is about to give birth to a baby in a makeshift tent because, as we are told several times, there is "no room" in the county hospital; they are "full up" (pp. 37, 40). The analogy to the Christmas story is obvious; Lisa's husband is named Joey, and the baby is a boy. However, the mysterious illuminated tent is invaded by the wily imposter Mac, who, like Satan, is capable of assuming many guises. Mac pretends to be a doctor and thus uses Lisa's condition to ingratiate himself with the pickers. Lying to London about his "medical experience," Mac successfully delivers the baby. Lisa's helpless silence is punctuated by only a few weak cries as she endures her first labor. Indeed, the voicelessness of Mrs. Nolan reverberates in the silence of the new mother, as well as in that of the old midwife, relegated to a dark corner of the tent. Reminiscent of Hecate, the moon goddess who, hearing Persephone's cries when raped, is a helpless double for Demeter,[23] the midwife, too, remains a passive witness to lawless violence. Even Mac says he thinks "that old woman knew lots more than I did. I think she knew it, too" (p. 42). As numerous critics have observed, Mac, supplanting the midwife, is the charlatan Communist party midwife who gives birth that night to the strike and perhaps also to Jim, his new young naive Communist disciple whose rebirth, according to John Timmerman, is "engineered by the party."[24]

Because Mac exploits, twists, and corrupts her pregnant condition, Lisa becomes the first of many individuals Mac views as useful objects; as such she illuminates Mac's inhumanity. Anthony Palmieri notes that he never looks at her as a human being giving birth to another life.[25] Instead, he says to Jim, "Course it was nice to help the girl, but hell, even if it killed her—we've got to use everything" (*IDB*, p. 42). Like Milton's Satan, a "wily adder, blithe and glad,"[26] Mac, in an ironic reversal or perversion of the Christmas myth, repeats "Jesus" and "Christ" several times and sees his delivery of Lisa's baby as part of a "story that will spread" (p. 43).

However, although Mac uses her for his own purposes, Lisa is one of Briffault's Mothers, an unquestionable and constant link with life and vital forces. Lisa disappears for five chapters while the strike is being started, not reappearing until after the fall—that is, old Dan's fall from the apple tree, which gives Mac an excuse to use another innocent human being to further his purposes. Lisa then reenters the novel as the "dark girl" (*IDB*, p. 137). Her darkness and namelessness having suggested her mysterious link with life, she now begins to emerge as an individual. We learn her name here, and it means "Dedicated to God." Ironically juxtaposed to the calculating utilitarianism of Mac, yet paradoxically echoing the near-religious fervor of Mac and Jim's dedication to their cause, she functions as a mythical presence, nearly always found in her father-in-law's tent—the command headquarters as it were, where Mac says he must think like a general (p. 244) and formulate battle strategies. The three main characters—Mac, Doc, and Jim—now react to Lisa, and in these reactions we may read their characters.

Before Lisa reenters the novel, Mac has forgotten her. Jim asks about "the girl's" condition, and Mac replies, "What girl?" There have been no others, but she is not on his mind. When Jim responds, "The girl with the baby," Mac remembers. "Oh, she's all right. But you'd think I was God the way London talks." Indeed. Mac not only plays God in this novel, but also exercises almost total control over the people he uses and despises, of whom Lisa is the first representative. "You know," he says to Jim, "she'll be a cute little broad when she gets some clothes and some make-up on. Make yourself another sandwich." Chewing his own sandwich he continues, "I never saw such a bunch of bags as this crowd. . . . Only decent one in the camp is thirteen years old. I'll admit she's got an eighteen-year-old can, but I'm doing no fifty years. . . . Every time the sun shines on my back all afternoon I get hot pants. What's wrong with that?" (*IDB*, p. 53). Jim does not answer. When Mac does look at Lisa, he sees her only in terms of sex. Later, after Doc Burton leaves and Mac misinterprets his interest in Lisa as sexual, he says, "Lisa, you're a lucky little twirp, you just had a kid [or] [y]ou'd have me in your hair," for Mac says he needs a woman to like him for a night, needs to "feel someone—with his skin" (p. 187). Lisa's pointed lack of response to Mac's words suggests Carol Gilligan's remarks on the "contrasts between male and female voices" that distinguish "between two entirely different modes of thought."[27] So different is Lisa from Mac that the two cannot communicate. They represent opposite worlds.

If Lisa elicits nothing but sexual innuendos from Mac, her effect on Doc is more complicated. Entering the tent where Jim, whose shoulder is wounded, sits with Lisa and Joey on the mattress, Doc remarks, "This looks like the holy family" (*IDB*, p. 175). He then asks Lisa to apply hot water to Jim's shoulder, for Jim is repeatedly described as "cold." Later, Doc sits on the mattress with Jim and Lisa and muses with sad eyes on the "brutal and meaningless" and complex nature of the coming battle with the fruit growers. Smiling at Lisa, he asks her what would bring her happiness. Her response is swift and sure. She would like a cow so she could have milk and make butter and cheese (pp. 183–84). She recalls happier times as a child when her father gave her milk and she would drink it "warm," straight from the cow. Here Lisa's words illustrate one of Gilligan's pivotal assumptions: "that the way people talk about their lives is of significance, that the language they use and the connections they make reveal the world that they see and in which they act."[28]

Lisa trusts Doc enough to talk with him, but the domesticity of her memories contrasts sharply with his recollections of the war; his attempts to mend the bodies of both German and American soldiers with chests "shot away" and legs "splintered off" made him desperately unhappy. Although their worlds are different, Doc and Lisa share a sensitivity to life that impels them to try to communicate their views to each other. Significantly, though, when Mac enters the tent, Doc rises to leave, reiterating, "I'm lonely, I guess; I'm awfully lonely. I'm working all alone, towards nothing. There's some compensation for you people. I only hear heartbeats through a stethoscope. You hear them in the air." Although Doc envies both Jim and Lisa, Jim's feeling of "pure religious ecstasy" (*IDB*, p. 185) in his allegiance to the party is a cold and deluded belief that leads only to death. The only one who really hears heartbeats is Lisa, who shuns violence and death, and Doc senses her life-affirming qualities. "Suddenly he leaned over and put his hand under Lisa's chin and raised her head up and looked into her shrinking eyes. Her hand came slowly up and pulled gently at his wrist. He let go and put his hand back in his pocket" (p. 186).

Lisa's goodness and warmth contrast with Doc's existential, scientific view of humanity, and she averts her eyes from him. Yet Doc at least looks at Lisa and recognizes her worth. Mac, not surprisingly, misinterprets the wordless dialogue between the two and tells Doc that he needs "some woman to go to" and that Dick, the "bedroom radical," can direct him to a brothel. Doc replies, "Sometimes you understand too much, Mac. Sometimes—nothing." Ultimately, however, he seems to sense that his and Lisa's worlds will never conflate: announcing that he will check on another patient (Al Anderson, yet another victim of the violence that has resulted since Mac and Jim's arrival), "Doc looked down at Lisa once more, and then he went out" (*IDB*, p. 186). We never see him again.

While Mac is not interested in Lisa, and Doc only dimly sees in her some mystery that eludes them all, Howard Levant, one of the few critics to look at Lisa, believes that "it is no accident that Lisa is paired nearly always with Jim."[29] Her point, he says, is "to imply the chance of love. Her indifference to the strike and her concentration on her baby are counterparts to Jim's inhuman avowal of violence."[30] Unlike her response to Dick, to whose blatantly allegorical sexuality she, like every woman who meets him, is attracted, Lisa's relation to Jim is one of genuine friendship, warmth, and goodwill. Mac asserts that both he and Jim are hated for their actions in the camp, but he is wrong: Lisa, although she feels uncomfortable with Mac's "cold-blooded" commitment to an inhuman cause and with Doc's scientific objective outlook, grows closer and closer to Jim as the story unfolds, and he to her. Jim, frequently described as cold, is attracted to her warmth. "You like me, don't you, Lisa?" he asks, and she replies in the affirmative (*IDB*, p. 246).

At one point, when Jim returns to his pup tent he is surprised to find her within, nursing the baby. Instinctively feeling safe with Jim and knowing that "he doesn't have a gun," she tells him she feels a bond with him, and admits somewhat guiltily that she enjoys nursing the baby. "It—ain't decent, do you think?" she asks (*IDB*, p. 156). One of the perversions in this dubious world in which she lives is that to enjoy caring for a baby appears shameful. Lisa here appears to illustrate psychologist Jean Baker Miller's point that men have tended to assume or devalue women's nurturing abilities; thus in Miller's words, "concern with relationships appears as a weakness of women rather than as a human strength."[31] Clearly, though, Lisa's entrance into Jim's tent is filled with possibilities, as is their chaste sharing of her mattress and exchanging of their thoughts. She wanders from tent to tent, silently demonstrating the possibilities of life and renewal, an image of fertility implicitly contrasted with an unnamed woman near the end of the novel who complains that she has a cancerous lump in her stomach (p. 216).

Lisa's goodness is obvious. Indeed, she nurses the young (her baby), the wounded (Jim), and the aged (old Dan). The fact that she nearly always appears in the command headquarters is significant; her presence there serves as a form of morality or conscience, and the men send her away whenever violence (Mac's ruthless and brutal beating of the high school boy) or death (Joy's corpse) appear in the tent. The death of Joy occurs after Dan falls from the apple tree, and his murder occurs just after Mac notes the absence of women in the area (*IDB*, p. 116). Again, Steinbeck appears deliberately to disassociate women from antilife forces. When Lisa's father-in-law sends her to the hospital tent where she eventually tends old Dan, she says softly, "I don't mind." Her eyes wet with tears, she stays with him even though she can smell his coming death. But when Joy's dead body is placed in the tent with her and her baby, Lisa, so connected with life, feels uncomfortable and leaves. Her business is with the living.

Although Lisa may be homeless, in her conversations with Jim her voice becomes increasingly assertive, confident, and revealing. Jim may be duped by the lies of Satan, but she most definitely is not. When Jim remarks to her that the men are "awfully quiet," she responds decisively, "They got their mouths full. . . . Always talkin', except their mouths' full. Always talkin'. If they got to fight, why don' they fight an' get it over, 'stead o' talkin'?" (*IDB*, p. 194). Jim, still in Mac's thrall, replies defensively, "This is a strike," and she retorts, "Even you talk all the time. . . . Talk don't turn no wheel" (p. 194). Lisa's voice is different, and she speaks her mind. Although their friendship grows in a garden of over four thousand acres of apples, Lisa is not an Eve figure: it is Jim, not she, who is seduced by the serpentlike Mac into thinking his vision of the white houses with picket fences and ripe gardens can be attained by Mac's dubious and devious means. Yet under her influence, Jim irresistibly draws nearer the feminine values that Lisa—and other women in the novel—represent: "I like to be near you," he tells her (p. 227).

A fascinating series of scenes near the end of the novel illuminates the magnetic appeal and the life-affirming, spiritual power of the women in Jim's life. Jim walks around the camp and sees another dark woman who

> stood in front of a tent, her head thrown back; and her throat was white. She combed her hair with long, beautiful sweeps of her arm. When Jim walked by she smiled wisely and said, "Good morning," and the combing didn't pause. Jim stopped. "No," she said. "Only good morning."
>   "You make me feel good," he said. (*IDB*, p. 218)

Moments later he will utter almost exactly the same words to the "dark girl" Lisa. Jim returns to the tent to tell Mac of the encounter and Mac, naturally, misinterprets the effect of the woman on Jim: "If I saw a decent looking woman, I'd go nuts," he says. But Jim ignores the innuendo and for the first and only time reveals his mother's covert visits to church with him. The memory is inextricably linked to the dark woman he has just seen outside the tent, who reminds him of the "Mary" in his mother's church:

> The smile on that woman—that's why I'm telling you this—Well, there was a Mary in there, and she had the same kind of smile, wise and cool and sure. One time I asked my mother why she smiled like that. My mother said, "She can smile because she's in Heaven." I think she was jealous, a little. . . . And one time I was there, looking at that Mary, and I saw a ring of little stars in the air, over her head, going around and around, like little birds. Really saw them, I mean. . . . They

made me feel happy, too. My old man would have been sore
if he knew. He never took any position that lasted. Everything
was wasted in him. (p. 219)

Notably, Jim's recollections of his mother's religiosity con-
tain references to neither God the Father nor to his son Jesus
Christ, and in her final silence Mrs. Nolan refuses even a
priest. Male figures are conspicuously missing. Mary, the wise
Mother, is the central figure, perhaps suggesting in Jim's sub-
conscious a merging of all women, perhaps including even the
ancient goddesses who preceded her. The powerful figure of
the mother-goddess Demeter is evoked here, as is that of
Athena, "wise," like the dark woman, the Mary figure, and
Mrs. Nolan.

Indeed, at this point in the novel, the images of the actual
women in Jim's life begin to merge with those of the mythical.
Much as in T. S. Eliot's *The Waste Land*, in which all the
women become one, Jim's words connect the nameless dark
woman with Mary and his nameless mother just before his
final conversation with the dark Lisa who, being much like a
sister to him, suggests his long-lost sister, May (the name
derives from Mary). Just after this vision Mac and Jim walk
into the orchard, and Jim has a revelation: "I never look at
anything," he blurts out. "I never take time to see anything.
It's going to be over, and I won't know—even how an apple
grows" (*IDB*, p. 239). Mac, meanwhile, is munching on a
"small, misshapen apple" (p. 238). Jim looks through the apple
trees and sees once again the "little white house, and its picket
fence." After visiting the house for what will be the last time,
Jim confesses that "something burned out of" him the night
his mother died (p. 242).

When they return to the tent, Jim and Lisa engage in their

final conversation. Their liking for each other contrasts with the imminent and dubious battle, after which neither knows where the other will be, again illustrating Gilligan's suggestion that the convergence of two different voices, male and female, "marks times of crisis and change."[32] Lisa's world is juxtaposed to that of the men, but as she and Jim draw closer together, their worlds become similar as, like him, she articulates the American dream. Jim and Lisa share a vision; each would like a little house with, in Lisa's words, a wood "floor and a toilet" not too far away (*IDB*, p. 192). He looks into her eyes and reminisces about a long-ago sun-drenched evening when a cat "turned gold for a minute." "'I like cats,' Lisa agreed softly. 'I had two cats onct, two of them.'" Lisa represents the ideal, the object of his quest, as well as the departed women in his life. As he and she recall together their domestic and aesthetic memories, they use almost the same language. But these verbal images constitute the last words they ever speak to each other and generate Jim's last look at Lisa, for Mac enters the tent with London—who "doesn't mind killing cats"—and once again dismisses her: "She looked sideways at Jim as she passed" (p. 247). Lisa, leaving with her baby, is a composite figure of mythical mothers, whether Mary or the earlier Greek ones, and her world moves irrevocably away from Jim as he is shot in the dark, dying on his knees in an attitude of prayer.

Gunned down, Jim dies the death of his father—and now, like Lisa, he becomes a useful object to Mac, who "picked Jim up and slung him over his shoulder, like a sack; and the dripping head hung down behind." As he displays Jim's faceless body, Mac is again like the serpent in the Garden: "He moved his jaws to speak, and seemed to break the frozen jaws loose" (*IDB*, p. 250), like a snake before it ingests some small animal. Lisa is absent from this final scene of death and violence.

In his novel of what Steinbeck called "man's eternal, bitter warfare with himself,"[33] the men prove woefully self-destructive and hence, as Gladstein points out, it is perhaps "appropriate" that Steinbeck's women appear "indestructible."[34] If the dubious battle is in fact Steinbeck's commentary on the Freudian—and masculine—concept of civilization and "progress,"[35] then the ending of Steinbeck's novel is bleak, indeed. The book's enormous unspeakable tension echoes through our own time, still unresolved a half-century later as we wage our own dark battles with the issues of gender, class, and race. If hope exists in this novel, it lies in the different world and different voice of the female embodied in Lisa. Like Ma Joad and Rose of Sharon, whom she clearly adumbrates, Lisa is not just part of "the people," but of the women, the feminine, the mothers, and the earth, and, one suspects, she will outlast the noise and the tumult raging around her.

4

CHARLOTTE COOK HADELLA

The Dialogic Tension in Steinbeck's Portrait of Curley's Wife

In November 1937 the stage play *Of Mice and Men* began its moderately successful New York run.[1] Midway in this run, Annie Laurie Williams, the play agent for McIntosh and Otis, reported to John Steinbeck that actress Claire Luce had some misgivings about her theatrical interpretation of Curley's wife. In a 1938 letter to Luce, Steinbeck suggested that he might help "clear [her] feelings" about the character if he could tell her what he knew about the girl,[2] but this letter, though cordial and apparently sincere, supplies few concrete details about the female in question. Nevertheless, the author's commentary reflects the same dialogic tension between the universality and the particularity of the woman that exists in the text of *Of Mice and Men*. Steinbeck's character sketch in the letter alternates between an authorial discourse that describes not a real person, but a character type, and a specific commentary that makes biographical references to an individual person. Briefly, the discourse even lapses into moral platitude, at which point Steinbeck apologizes for "preaching" to his reader (*SLL*, p. 154). The author's difficulty in describing Curley's wife beyond her existence in the play script signals the power of context over text that shapes the characterization of the woman in Steinbeck's fiction.

For the term "dialogic tension," I am borrowing from Mikhail Bakhtin's theory of discourse as dialogue between a speaker and a listener, about a hero or subject.[3] In the rhetorical triangle of speaker-listener-subject, Bakhtin substitutes "hero" for "subject" and views hero as active agent, interacting with the speaker "to shape language and determine form. At times, the hero becomes the dominant influence in verbal and written utterance."[4] Dialogic tension exists in all discourse because words, the elements of the dialogue, are loaded with various social nuances that influence each other and perhaps even change as a result of the association. Bakhtin recognizes subject as an active agent in discourse that helps to explain the power of context over text: "Each word tastes of the context and contexts in which it has lived its socially charged life: all words and forms are populated by intentions. Contextual overtones . . . are inevitable in the word."[5]

From this rhetorical perspective, then, Steinbeck's letter provides critical clues to the characterization of Curley's wife in *Of Mice and Men;* it reveals the author's difficulty in finding his own words to describe the character once he has taken her out of the context of the story, where she is characterized by what others say about her and by her own actions and speech. Also, the varied levels of discourse that interact to create dialogic tension are easier to discern in the letter than in the fiction because the letter features one "speaker" only, as opposed to a cast of characters. Still, we hear at least three voices: an objective voice that relates what the woman's social context dictates about her character, a more personal voice in which Steinbeck talks about the particular woman he had in mind when he created the character, and an emotional speaker who demands sympathy from his listener for the person he is describing.

In the letter, these "voices" are fairly distinct as the author tries to inform his reader about Curley's wife as she exists outside the context of the story. Steinbeck writes: "About the girl—I don't know of course what you think about her, but perhaps if I should tell you a little about her as I know her, it might clear your feeling about her" (*SLL*, p. 154). Then the explanation of Curley's wife to Luce begins with broad generalizations about the girl's background expressed in the diction of a social worker. She had been nurtured in "an atmosphere of fighting and suspicion," yet she maintained a "natural trustfulness" that constantly led to disappointment (p. 154). Her rigid moral training had taught her "that she must remain a virgin because that was the only way she could get a husband" (p. 154). Having been "trained by threat," she learned to be hard, especially when she was frightened (p. 154). This passage, though sympathetic in tone, supplies no specific personal details about the girl to whom Steinbeck is referring. Consequently, the description sounds like an analysis of a personality type, more like a paragraph from a psychology textbook than a description of a person whom the author claims to know. Presumably, the actress would already have been able to draw general conclusions such as the ones mentioned here after weeks of delivering such lines as, "Nobody never got to me before I was married. I was straight. I tell you I was good. I was. You know Curley. You know he wouldn't stay with me if he wasn't sure."[6]

In fact, Curley's wife reveals more specific details about

herself in the play script of *Of Mice and Men* than Steinbeck supplies for Luce anywhere in the letter. Expanding the role of Curley's wife was one of the major revisions that Steinbeck made when he transformed the novella into a play. The lines that Curley's wife speaks in the barn just before Lennie strokes her hair and breaks her neck reveal specific details of her family background. Her father was a sign painter and an alcoholic; violent arguments between her parents were a daily occurrence. The girl describes a childhood episode in which her father tried to run away with her, but the authorities stopped him and "put him away." She ends the speech with "I wish we'd went" (*OMM*, p. 371). These details not only ground the character in a specific past, but also allow the audience to hear the woman's voice when she is not engaged in the sexual repartee that characterizes most of her utterances. This passage helps to explain, as well, why the young woman ever considered a life with someone like Curley to be desirable. That the girl speaks sincerely to Lennie only, an inattentive and uncomprehending listener, indicates that Steinbeck wishes to humanize her character for the audience while maintaining her nonperson status with those characters in the play who are supposedly capable of human understanding.

The character description in the letter continues, but Steinbeck, as if realizing that he was not telling his reader anything about the character that she could not discern for herself from lines in the play, shifts in midparagraph to present-tense observations that seem relatively more particular than his opening statements. "She is a nice, kind girl and not a floozy" (*SLL*, p. 154), he explains. "No man has ever considered her as anything except a girl to try to make. She has never talked to a man except in the sexual fencing conversation. She is not highly sexed particularly but knows instinctively that if she is to be noticed at all, it will be because some one [sic] finds her sexually desirable" (pp. 154–55). This segment of the description, though only slightly more specific than the passage previously cited, is certainly more subjective. Here Steinbeck has moved from analyzing the girl's environment to specifying the particularly sexual nature of all her social experiences. However, by insisting upon the verbal distinction between what the girl is ("nice" and "kind") and what she is not (a "floozy"), Steinbeck indicates his own uncertainty about his audience's perception of the character. This apparent uncertainty arises from the disagreement between the discourse of the evil-woman stereotype that permeates the play script and the author's presentation of the character through situation, action, speech, and symbol.

Since the subject of *Of Mice and Men*, on one level at least, is the destructive power of illusion as it pertains particularly to the American Dream, mythical discourse naturally influences the story. Critics have noted that the Garden of Eden myth "looms large" in *Of Mice and Men*,[7] and Steinbeck appropriates Edenic elements to convey his personal interpretation of the American Dream. The role of woman in the Edenic framework, of course, is that of the temptress, the despoiler of the Garden. That Steinbeck manipulates his story to encompass the mythical interpretation is clear. In a *New York Times* interview in December 1937, while discussing his sources for characters and incidents in *Of Mice and Men*, Steinbeck claimed that he had witnessed Lennie's real-life counterpart's killing of a man, not a woman: "I was a bindle-stiff myself for quite a spell. I worked in the same country that the story is laid in. The characters are composites to a certain extent. Lennie was a real person. He's in an insane asylum in California right now. I worked alongside him for many weeks. He didn't kill a girl. He killed a ranch foreman. Got sore because the boss had fired his pal and stuck a pitchfork right through his stomach. I hate to tell you how many times. I saw him do it. We couldn't stop him until it was too late."[8]

To fit the mythical framework of his story, Steinbeck changes Lennie's victim from a man to a woman. Although George and Lennie's illusion of an Edenic existence would have been shattered just as surely if Lennie had killed Curley, for instance, instead of Curley's wife, Steinbeck makes the woman the instrument of destruction of the land dream. The mythical discourse of the fiction dictates that a woman precipitate the exile from paradise. Consequently, George espouses this concept of womanhood and accepts Candy's assessment of Curley's wife as a "tart" before he ever meets her in person (*OMM*, p. 322).

Steinbeck, however, counters George's stereotypical condemnation of the woman by undermining the entire scenario of the Garden myth; he intimates that the paradise of the land dream is doomed before Curley's wife ever enters the story. Critics generally agree that the grove in the opening scene, where George and Lennie spend the night before reporting to work at the ranch—the same grove in which George shoots Lennie at the end of the story—symbolizes the dream of owning the farm and "living off the fat of the land" (*OMM*, p. 309). But when Lennie gulps the water from the pool in the grove, George warns him that it might make him sick. "I ain't sure it's good water [George said]. Looks kinda scummy to me" (p. 300). George's comment reveals that, symbolically at least, paradise may already be spoiled. Moreover, later in the play, when George talks about the actual farm that he intends to buy for himself and Lennie, he explains to Candy that he can get the place for a really cheap price, "for six hundred bucks.

The ole people that owns it is flat bust" (p. 347). Apparently, the present owners of George's dream farm are not able to live "off the fat of the land," a detail that both he and Candy conveniently overlook. By deliberately bringing this fact to the attention of the audience, Steinbeck creates a tension between George's mythical discourse of the dream life toward which he is striving and the voice of reality, which says that even if George acquired the piece of land that he has in mind, his dream of an Edenic existence would still not be realized.

Likewise, even as Steinbeck attempts to clarify Luce's understanding of the character she must portray, his explication is complicated by the same dialogic tension between universality and particularity that exists in the fiction. Finally, abandoning any pretense of specific, concrete description of Curley's wife in his letter, Steinbeck writes: "If you knew her, if you could ever break down the thousand little defenses she had built up, you would find a nice person, an honest person, and you would end up by loving her. But such a thing can never happen" (*SLL*, p. 155). What can and does happen in *Of Mice and Men*, which was originally titled "Something That Happened,"[9] is that no one loves Curley's wife. She does not even love herself. Revisions in the story for the play script, however, indicate that Steinbeck was aware of the woman's lack of self-esteem in the novel and attempted to add an assertive dimension to her character in the play. For instance, when she runs into Lennie in the barn, she has come there to hide her suitcase. She intends to leave Curley as soon as she can sneak away and hitchhike to Hollywood. Instead of merely voicing her dissatisfaction with life on the ranch, she takes specific action; she plans an escape. Even in pursuit of her personal vision, however, the woman has no solid notion of herself as a worthwhile person. Her dream is to be in pictures—to become a cinematic image that occupies no space in the real world. She even imagines that the clothes she would wear in the movies would be the ones she would wear all the time. Thus she will always be just an image, the woman from the silver screen.

Steinbeck's emotional appeal to Luce, "If you knew her . . . you would end up by loving her," underscores the author's frustration with the task of explaining a character out of context whose major function in her fictional text is to be misunderstood, undiscovered as a human being, unknown even to herself. These few lines also reveal Steinbeck's aware-ness of privileged authorial information that he is unable to impart to his reader. The "you," of course, in Steinbeck's injunction to the actress, is not directed at Luce in particular, but addresses an American society generally in which vulner-able, unfortunate young women must survive. Steinbeck adds, "I hope you won't think I'm preaching," a comment that indicates that he was conscious of, perhaps even embarrassed by, the intense moral tone of his appeal.

The character description in the letter closes with that same peculiar mixture of particularity and universality with which Steinbeck began the sketch: "I've known this girl and I'm just trying to tell you what she is like. She is afraid of everyone in the world. You've known girls like that, haven't you? You can see them in Central Park on a hot night. They travel in groups for protection. They pretend to be wise and hard and volup-tuous" (*SLL*, p. 155).

Pretend is the operative verb here, and it is upon this question of pretended evil versus innate evil that an assess-ment of Curley's wife depends. A brief sampling of criti-cal comments from the past three decades suggests that Steinbeck's readers draw various conclusions. Peter Lisca, in his 1958 study, *The Wide World of John Steinbeck*, analyzes recurring motifs of language, action, and symbol in the novel and identifies Curley's wife as a "mice symbol . . . who threatens [George and Lennie's] dream by bringing with her the harsh realities of the outside world and by arousing Lennie's interest."[10] This statement follows Lisca's discussion of inevitability in the novel. To Lennie, the rabbits, and by extension all soft, furry things, represent the dream of owning the farm. But the dead mouse in the first scene of the story signals the inevitable failure of the dream. Lennie destroys soft, furry things—as his killings of mice and of the puppy indicate. Thus, Curley's wife is just another soft, furry thing doomed to destruction by Lennie. Her death is just the "something" that was bound to happen to ensure the shattering of George and Lennie's illusion. Lisca's assessment of the woman is relatively neutral: she brings "the harsh realities of the outside world" to bear upon the events of the story, but she does not necessarily represent evil.[11]

On the other hand, in 1974 both Mark Spilka and Howard Levant offered scathing interpretations of Curley's wife. According to Spilka, "Steinbeck projects his own hostilities [toward the woman] through George and Lennie. He has himself given this woman no other name but 'Curley's wife,' as if she had no personal identity for him. He has presented her, in the novel, as vain, provocative, vicious . . . and only incidentally lonely."[12] Steinbeck's revision of the woman's role in the play, Spilka wrote, "creates a new imbalance to correct an old one. His sentimentality is the obverse side of his hostility. . . . Only when sexually quiescent—as in death or childhood—can [Curley's wife] win this author's heart."[13] Similarly, Levant observed that the woman "is characterless, nameless, and constantly discontent, so her death inspires none of the sympathy one might feel for a kind or serene woman."[14]

In a 1979 article that analyzes Steinbeck's treatment of women in his plays, Sandra Beatty suggests that Curley's wife "serves to reinforce the theme of loneliness, isolation, and the idea of a personal dream which is central to the play. She commands both our sympathy and respect because of her naive yet genuine pursuit of a life-long dream."[15] Beatty believes that Steinbeck, by not giving the female character a name, "deliberately delineat[ed] her role insofar as it is seen by the male characters in the play."[16] Along this same line, Louis Owens, in *John Steinbeck's Re-Vision of America*, reasons that woman is not the evil in the mythical garden of *Of Mice and Men*. Owens proposes that "the real serpent is loneliness and the barriers between men and women that create and reinforce this loneliness."[17] Thus Steinbeck allows Curley's wife to share in the "yearning all men have for warm, living contact."[18]

Though all of these critics are analyzing the same character, the differences in the conclusions drawn about her are obvious. These conflicts may be attributed to the levels of discourse in the story that compete for definition, for privileged acceptance by the listener. The fiction does not offer an authoritative or absolute statement on the woman's character. It is not surprising, then, that Claire Luce, wishing to portray the woman in the way that the playwright had conceived of her, had misgivings about her interpretation of Curley's wife. That Steinbeck sincerely tried to satisfy the actress's request for information is apparent, but it is equally clear that his letter could not have helped Luce substantially. By countering his stated conviction that to know this character would be to love her with the forlorn declaration that such a thing could never happen, Steinbeck gives us perhaps the most authoritative statement that he can about Curley's wife. What he reveals in that emotional outburst is that neither the context of the play nor the context of the woman's life allows her full humanity; for this reason, her portrait is incomplete. Nevertheless, even decades after its inception, Steinbeck's little story about something that happened has something to tell its audience, not just of mice and men, but also of *women* who may find themselves in a world where they are unknown and therefore unloved.

Part II

The Years of Greatness
Steinbeck's Worker Trilogy

5

LOUIS OWENS

Writing "in Costume"
The Missing Voices of *In Dubious Battle*

"Source study," Stephen J. Greenblatt has declared, "is the elephants' graveyard of literary history." After making this declaration, Greenblatt goes on in the same essay to conduct an impressive examination of a major source for Shakespeare's *King Lear*, adding this note: "For me the study of the literary is the study of contingent, particular, intended, and historically embedded works."[1]

What I am attempting here is to tiptoe around the elephants' graveyard while looking a bit more closely at John Steinbeck's novel *In Dubious Battle* as a "contingent, particular, intended, and historically embedded" work. In doing so, I think it is useful to glance at a sort of countertext by one of Steinbeck's slightly younger contemporaries, Filipino-American writer Carlos Bulosan.

Bulosan, in an essay entitled "My Education," published in 1979, described his long, arduous quest to become a writer and an American. He had arrived in America in 1930 as a naive seventeen-year-old with fewer than three years of formal schooling. Soon, however, he had taught himself to read English and had read everything he could get his hands on. "I had a preliminary knowledge of American history to guide me," he wrote. "I had read *Gone with the Wind*, and saw the extent of the lie that corrupted the American dream. I read Dreiser, Anderson, Lewis, and their younger contemporaries: Faulkner, Hemingway, Caldwell, Steinbeck. I had hoped to find in these writers a weapon strong enough to blast the walls that imprisoned the American soul. But they were merely describing the disease—they did not reveal any evidence that they knew how to eradicate it."[2] Bulosan went on to be more specific: "Hemingway was too preoccupied with himself, and consequently he wrote of himself and his frustrations. I was also disappointed with Faulkner. Why did he give form to decay? And Caldwell, Steinbeck—why did they write in costume?"[3]

As a critic with a special interest in Steinbeck, I noted the similarity here to Steinbeck's statement about Faulkner: "The festered characters of Faulkner are not very interesting to me," he declared, "unless their festers are heroic."[4] Bulosan's statement concerning Steinbeck, however, especially caught my eye. What did he mean by writing "in costume"? I decided to examine the Steinbeck work that would undoubtedly have interested Bulosan the most, and the one that seemed to touch upon Bulosan's life most closely: *In Dubious Battle*, published in 1936.

When he stepped off a ship in Seattle on July 22, 1930, Bulosan, like countless other immigrants, had his heart set on the American Dream. What he found, instead, was hardship and exploitation in the fields and orchards of the West Coast—exploitation promoted by a disturbing degree of officially sanctioned racism. What he found, of course, was an old story to the waves of immigrants—Chinese, Mexican, Japanese, Hindu, and Filipino—who had been coming to the West

Coast in search of employment already for more than half a century.

Almost as soon as he arrived in America, Bulosan became caught up in the increasingly violent conflict between labor and corporate agriculture in the West. Within a decade he would be a seasoned labor organizer as well as an emerging American writer, though he would never succeed in becoming an American citizen. Embroiled in the thick of California farm labor disputes, Bulosan would travel up and down the state, always working for his fellow laborers and simultaneously trying to teach himself to read and write. In 1945 he would publish *America Is in the Heart*,[5] an autobiography detailing his experiences. Interestingly, one of the towns that figures most heavily in Bulosan's chronicles is Salinas, Steinbeck's birthplace.

Aside from his declaration that Steinbeck wrote "in costume," what does Bulosan have to do with Steinbeck and, in particular, *In Dubious Battle*? The most obvious connection lies in the fact that both Steinbeck and Bulosan wrote about agricultural labor organizers and strikers in California during the thirties. More significantly, each writer's work contains a portrait of a neophyte labor organizer. Jim Nolan, in Steinbeck's *In Dubious Battle*, and Bulosan, himself, throughout much of his *America Is in the Heart*, both fit this category. And the two neophytes share remarkable similarities.

Initially both Bulosan and Jim were young, rather innocent, and remarkably free of vices. Both lacked significant formal education, but in spite of this both were, or became, astonishingly well read. Jim tells a party recruiter in the novel: "I've read a lot. . . . One day I met a man in the park. He made a list of things for me to read."[6] The man in the park's list included Plato, Kant, Hegel, Carlyle, Spinoza, Nietzsche, and Marx, among others. Bulosan had no fortuitous meeting with a literary angel in a park, but he was hospitalized for two years while undergoing three operations for tuberculosis. During these two years, a well-educated young lady named Eileen Odell brought him a steady stream of books. "Throughout the year," Bulosan wrote, "I read one book a day including Sundays" (*AIH*, p. 245). Included in his reading were not only writers such as Kafka, Lorca, Faulkner, Steinbeck, Whitman, and Robert Briffault (*Rational Evolution*), but also such leftist publications as *New Masses, Partisan Review,* and *New Republic* (p. 266).

Both Bulosan and Jim grew up amidst oppression. While Jim watched his father being destroyed in his one-man war against capitalism, Bulosan saw his peasant father and mother crushed by the absentee landlord system in the Philippines and his family fragmented. Both Jim and Bulosan witnessed and experienced further brutalities in their struggles against capitalism. So traumatic was Bulosan's experience that at one point he wrote, "The terrible truth in America shatters the Filipino's dream of fraternity" (*AIH*, p. xiii). Both Jim and Bulosan were lonely and cut off until they discovered fulfillment in working for a larger cause. Jim, who admits that he was lonely before, declares once he is working for the "cause": "I never felt so good before. I'm all swelled up with a good feeling" (*IDB*, p. 35). And before joining in the brotherhood of organized labor, Bulosan said of the outcast Filipino in America: "He is the loneliest thing on earth" (*AIH*, p. xiii). The matrices within which both characters are formed seem similar. The evolved characters of Jim Nolan and Carlos Bulosan, however, are very distinct.

As every alert reader soon discovers, the plot of *In Dubious Battle* turns upon a rather heavy irony. Jim Nolan, lonely and cut off as the novel opens, grows in the course of the story to feel an overpowering sense of belonging to the "cause." However, while Jim is moving closer to this euphoric sense of belonging to something larger than himself, he is becoming progressively dehumanized.

This level of irony functions, in part, to isolate the single impulse upon which Steinbeck wished to focus: man's need to belong to something larger than the isolated self, even if that something is as dubious as the cause depicted in the novel. It is the belonging, pure and simple, that brings Jim happiness. It is most clearly not whatever good Jim is doing or may do for his fellow man.

Steinbeck explained his own interest in this novel in an oft-quoted letter to George Albee: "I have used a small strike in an orchard valley as the symbol of man's eternal, bitter warfare with himself. I'm not interested in strike as means of raising men's wages, and I'm not interested in ranting about justice and oppression, mere outcroppings which indicate the condition. But man hates something in himself. He has been able to defeat every natural obstacle but himself he cannot win over unless he kills every individual. And this self-hate which goes so closely in hand with self-love is what I wrote about," (*SLL*, p. 98). Steinbeck went on in this same letter to say, "I wanted to be merely a recording consciousness, judging nothing, simply putting down the thing" (p. 98).

Thus, although Steinbeck admitted that he had initially planned "to write a journalistic account of a strike," his ultimate interest in this novel was not social realism but rather an attempt to find what he, in another letter discussing "group man," called "a fictional symbolism which will act as a vehicle" (*SLL*, p. 75). Steinbeck's disinterest in social realism is further attested to by his statement to Carl Wilhelmson in August

1933: "I don't think you will like my latest work. It leaves realism farther and farther behind. I never had much ability for nor faith nor belief in realism" (p. 87). In another letter to Wilhelmson, dated April 1936 and referring to the just-published *In Dubious Battle*, Steinbeck again dismissed realism and said, "The Battle with its tricks to make a semblance of reality wasn't very close."[7]

In spite of his disavowal of realism, however, at other moments Steinbeck insisted emphatically upon the accuracy of representation in this novel. In a letter to Albee, he said, "I must put in the beginning of this book a guarantee that all persons, places and events are fictional because it all has happened and I don't want anybody hurt because of my retelling" (*SLL*, p. 99). In a letter to his agent, Mavis McIntosh, in response to Covici-Friede's initial rejection of the novel, he insisted, "In this book I was making nothing up" (p. 107). Ironically, Covici-Friede's short-lived rejection had stemmed from a Marxist editor's doubts about the book's accuracy. According to Jackson J. Benson, "Steinbeck was furious, not so much that the book had been rejected, but that some 'cocktail circuit' communist back in New York had accused him of being inaccurate when detailed accuracy was exactly what he had prided himself on in preparing the manuscript."[8]

That Steinbeck was, in fact, far from faithful to the reality of labor strife in California's fields and orchards is not news. In an essay published in 1980, Benson and Anne Loftis documented Steinbeck's variations from historical fact, a clarification Benson repeats in his 1984 biography of Steinbeck. Among other inconsistencies, Benson and Loftis pointed out that "although three-quarters of the workers on both the peach and cotton strikes [the strikes that served as models for Steinbeck's fictional strike] were Mexican, all the workers in *In Dubious*

Battle are white."[9] These critics noted furthermore that whereas in Steinbeck's novel the active strikers are all male, in the real strikes Steinbeck had in mind as models "a considerable amount of strike activity was carried out by women."[10] Perhaps it is more important, as Benson and Loftis indicate, that the key Communist party organizers involved in the peach and cotton strikes, Caroline Decker and Pat Chambers (the latter may have served as a model for Mac in the novel), seem to have cared deeply about the immediate welfare of the individual strikers.

Another of Steinbeck's variations from historical accuracy might have struck Bulosan with particular force, for there are no Filipinos in *In Dubious Battle*. Carey McWilliams, author of *Factories in the Fields* and authority on the subject of California farm labor during this period, documented the key role that the Filipino played in California's strikes, particularly in the Salinas Valley, which has come to be called "Steinbeck Country." McWilliams wrote: "The Filipino is a real fighter and his strikes have been dangerous. In August, 1934, about 3,000 Filipino workers went on strike . . . near Salinas, California. An army of special deputies descended on the Filipino picket line and herded a group of about 700 Filipinos together and drove them from the community. As a part of this campaign, a Filipino labor camp was raided and burned to the ground."[11] McWilliams pointed out that a concentration camp was erected near Salinas in 1936, and "when local workers inquired of the shippers-growers why such a curious construction had been established, they were told that it was built 'to hold strikers, but of course we won't put white men in it, just Filipinos.'"[12] Even the later lettuce strikes in Salinas in September 1936, after the influx of Dust Bowl migrants had swelled the ranks of white farm laborers (and after *In Dubious*

Battle had been published), included three thousand white workers and five hundred Filipinos.[13]

While Filipinos were holding center stage in some of the bloodiest labor clashes in Salinas, Steinbeck was making frequent visits to Salinas from nearby Pacific Grove to sit with his dying father.[14] It is difficult to believe that Steinbeck was not aware of the key role Filipinos were playing in the labor disputes. Given the depth of Bulosan's political engagement, the omission of his fellow Filipinos might well have struck him as a deliberate ideological decision by Steinbeck.

Given the overwhelming presence of Mexican workers in California's strikes, however, the omission of that minority must have been even more surprising. In the 1936 celery strikes, according to McWilliams, 93.6 percent of the strikers were Mexican; only 6.8 percent were white.[15] An interesting sidelight here is the fact that between 1931 and 1934, hostility against foreign workers in the United States—primarily in California—climaxed with the deportation or repatriation of up to one-third of the Mexican population, even though many of these workers had been born in the United States. Most Americans are not aware of the amazing fact that, as the exodus of refugees Steinbeck would describe in *The Grapes of Wrath* was lining Route 66 westward toward the Golden State, another even more ragged caravan was crawling along U.S. 101 southward from California to Mexico.[16] But even with as much as a third of their population deported and the influx of white migrant workers increasing, Mexican and Mexican-American farm workers still dominated much of the agricultural labor scene in California in the mid- and late thirties, just as they do today.

Bulosan might have wondered also why Steinbeck chose to portray the agricultural worker so grimly. There is certainly no doubt that the strikers of *In Dubious Battle* are an unadmirable lot, very nearly personifying all of the Seven Deadly Sins. Old Dan, the aged topfaller, compares his fellow workers to dogs fighting over a bone, and Jim Nolan calls them "swine." Doc Burton sums up this dark picture of humanity when he says, "Psychologists say a man's self-love is balanced neatly with self-hate. Mankind must be the same. We fight ourselves and we can only win by killing every man." This follows immediately upon Doc's declaration, "How man hates himself" (*IDB*, p. 184).

Benson has suggested that Steinbeck created such a dark view of his strikers because portraying "the actual heroism of his models would have been impossible—too many Marxist melodramas had been written over the years that automatically cast the labor leaders as heroes and the capitalists as villains. Anything that smacked of this same routine would have been perceived as propaganda."[17] This explanation of the author's motivation suggests that Steinbeck's distortion may have been the result of a subtle rhetorical strategy designed to avoid rejection of his novel by critics and popular readers. Such a supposition would emphasize a sophisticated sensitivity to audience as described by Mikhail Bakhtin, who wrote: "Every discourse presupposes a special conception of the listener, of his apperceptive background and the degree of his responsiveness."[18] If we make such a supposition here, we can also assume that Steinbeck cleverly distorted reality to make his fiction conform to his anticipated readers' preconceptions of what that reality should be. Because the "unreal" novel conforms to their preconceptions, the critics/readers label the novel "realistic." In the end, given this line of reasoning, Steinbeck, by diverging so drastically from the reality of his models, almost comically outwitted his critics.

Unless a lost Steinbeck letter turns up to explain it in the author's words, we will most likely never know Steinbeck's intention in creating a strike so at odds with what we know of the strikes that actually occurred. We can only speculate. My guess would be that Steinbeck—who never wrote to please critics—devalued the heroism and humanity of his strike leaders and omitted the crucial roles of women and ethnic minorities from this novel, not to make his work more "realistic" or believable, but because his main concern was to illustrate his current pet theory about "group-man," and he did not want this illustration blurred. To show heroic individuals operating out of concern for other individuals would have complicated the simple picture of group-man he wished to show, and to have introduced the complexities of race and gender would have blurred the single focus sought.

Regardless of Steinbeck's motivation in portraying this battleground so darkly, it is interesting to contrast both Doc Burton's theorizing about self-hatred and Steinbeck's at best ungenerous portrayal of the strikers with a statement by Bulosan. "I knew, even then," he wrote of his darkest hour as a labor activist, "that it was not natural, indeed, to run from goodness and beauty" (*AIH*, p. 184). Steinbeck and Doc Burton would seem to believe that it is indeed, in some perverse way, natural for man to hate himself and to turn away from goodness and beauty as part of this self-loathing. Bulosan had experienced mob violence repeatedly as he was beaten and saw friends tortured and even killed by "vigilantes." And, perhaps as a result of his experiences with mobs, Bulosan, like Steinbeck, became interested in the behavior of the group, or collective whole. McWilliams said of Bulosan: "Perhaps because he had suffered so much, Carlos could not endure the thought of suffering in others. . . . He tried to understand and interpret chaos and cruelty 'from a collective point of view, because it was pervasive and universal. . . . ' He loved all living things and was determined to maintain a generous view of the species" (pp. xviii–xix). In spite of his generous view of the species and his refusal to run from goodness and beauty, Bulosan was aware also of the beast within, the same beast that emerges in *In Dubious Battle* and roars its thirst for blood. Thinking of the "invisible scars" he bore from years of labor struggle, Bulosan said, "I was terribly afraid of myself, for it was the beast, the monster, the murderer of love and kindness that would raise its dark head to defy all that was good and beautiful in life" (pp. 135–36).

In Dubious Battle ends on the darkest note in Steinbeck's fiction. Doc has disappeared, "grabbed" and most likely murdered by vigilantes. The strike is doomed to a bloody failure. Throughout the camp men are suffering terribly—old Dan, whose broken hip was the trigger for the strike, is delirious with pain; a striker is screaming with an untreated broken ankle; and Burke lies in a tent with his jaw torn almost off by London's fist. There is neither food nor hope. Jim Nolan has been killed by vigilantes, his face blown away by a shotgun blast, and Mac stands before the strikers with Jim's horrifying corpse spotlighted, inciting the bloodthirsty mob to greater, and more mindless, violence.

It is a dubious battle, indeed. And with Mac's, and the novel's, final words, Steinbeck brazenly refused to resolve the tensions he created. "Comrades!" Mac intones, "He didn't want nothing for himself." Except for the signal "Comrades!" Mac's final statement echoes verbatim what he said earlier about Joy, also sacrificed for the cause. The ideologically dense signifier "Comrades!" and the sense of rote repetition ironically serve to undervalue Mac's tribute to Jim, casting a faint

but unmistakably cynical shadow across Mac's rhetorical pos-
turing. At the same time, and paradoxically, the reader is aware
both that Mac feels deeply the truth of his words and that Mac
cared deeply for Jim. On still another level, however, the
reader is aware, though Mac may not be, that Jim did want
something for himself. It was the good feeling that came from
belonging to the "cause" that prompted Jim's actions, not any
isolated commitment to humanity. Jim succumbed to a type of
martyr complex, the overwhelming desire to be "used," because it both bound him to the "whole" and made him feel
better than he had ever felt before. In this sense everything Jim
did was for himself, to gratify his desire for fulfillment and
euphoria. The verbatim repetition also underscores, of course,
the reader's growing recognition that what has happened is
part of an ongoing and endless (epic) pattern—what Steinbeck
and Doc Burton would define as man's eternal, bitter warfare
with himself.

Mac's final words also serve as a fascinating example of what
Bakhtin terms "heteroglossia," or "double-voiced discourse."[19]
In commenting upon the death of Joy earlier in the novel, Mac
had said, "He was such a good little guy. . . . He didn't want
nothing for himself" (IDB, pp. 148–49). This comment is made
during a private moment, with Jim as the only audience. The
impression Steinbeck gives is that this is Mac's heartfelt response to his friend's death, an example of what Bakhtin terms
"internally persuasive discourse." When Mac repeats the same
words about Jim, Mac is in dialogue with himself, and in
repetition his own words have taken on a hint of what Bakhtin
calls "authoritative discourse," or "privileged language" that
approaches us from without.[20] The result is a double-voiced
utterance that appears to unite, within Mac, both "the authority of discourse and its internal persuasiveness."[21] This hybrid-

ization is introduced by the introductory epithet of "Comrades!"; the word arrives with the full weight of authoritative discourse behind it. This is what Bakhtin calls a "prior discourse," one that bears an authority "already acknowledged in the past."[22] Between introductory epithet and double-voiced utterance, through Mac's and the novel's last words, Steinbeck—perhaps America's unsurpassed master of what Bakhtin defined as dialogism in the novel—has brilliantly highlighted the irresolvable tensions embodied in the work.

Once we have recognized Steinbeck's brilliant achievement here, we should note also what he failed to do. According to Bakhtin, discourse in the novel consists of a kind of battleground between centripetal and centrifugal forces in language and culture. Language itself can be social, or peculiar to different social strata within a society; it can be national, as in English, Spanish; and it can be alien, or other, any language not one's own.[23] Few writers have worked more effectively within the complexities of social language than did Steinbeck, and we see that sensibility operating in *In Dubious Battle*, emphasized when Doc Burton notes that Mac's language undergoes chameleonlike changes to match whatever social stratum in which he finds himself. The "otherness" of language is exemplified in the authoritative discourse of the "party."

What Steinbeck omitted from this novel, however, is the complexity of national languages, with their concomitant social discourses. According to McWilliams, so great was the diversity of national languages among the actual strikers that the bookkeeper of one of the large farm-factories in California's San Joaquin Valley "had to be a trained linguist," dealing "with four or five racial groups."[24] In the Corcoran strikers' camp that Steinbeck used as a model for his fictional camp, the population and importance of Mexican strikers was so significant that at one point, McWilliams wrote, "Mr. Enrique Bravo, the Mexican Consul, spoke [to the camp] and warned the Mexicans that 'grave international complications' might result if they did not abandon the strike."[25] In limiting his strikers to a linguistically homogenous mass of white, lower-class American males, Steinbeck simply ignored the true polyglossia of the phenomenon he was describing. One result of his decision to leave out the complexities of culture, race, gender, and language found in his actual models is that his achievement in this novel serves rather paradoxically as a centripetal force, in contrast to the primarily "decentralizing" energy Bakhtin identifies in the genre of the novel. That is, Steinbeck's fictional picture serves to reinforce the ideology of the dominant social stratum in the country in the 1930s, a stratum composed primarily of white males. The "other" outcast populations of the nation—women and ethnic minorities—are further excluded from the national discourse in which they played such a crucial historical role.

Benson and Loftis expressed the paradoxical irony of this novel very perceptively, saying, "We cannot fault Steinbeck for being convincing, nor can we blame him for having chosen from his sources what he wished for his own purposes. . . . That this depiction of hell, this parable of man's self-hatred, should still be thought of as one of our most journalistically truthful novels is an ironic comment on our times, our taste, and the relationships of our literature to our historical perceptions."[26]

It goes without saying that we cannot fault Steinbeck for manipulating the raw materials of his fiction in any way he saw fit. His goal was primarily an aesthetic one, and the critical and popular acceptance of *In Dubious Battle* indicates that he succeeded impressively. But there are questions we should perhaps ask about the causes and effects of this "historically embedded" novel. For example, what does it mean to be "merely a recording consciousness, judging nothing, simply putting down the thing"?

In his short story "Johnny Bear," Steinbeck created a paradigm of the artist in the character of Johnny Bear, who is a "recording device" playing back to an audience exactly what he hears. There is apparently neither distortion nor authorial interference in the material Johnny Bear places before his outraged and interested audience; he simply puts down "the thing." Suppose, however, that Johnny only pretended to be a half-wit "objective" author and cleverly decided to alter the recorded reality in conformity with certain preconceived hypotheses he had about mankind or womankind? Johnny might, for example, have a fascination with something he called a "phalanx" theory. And suppose further that Johnny also pragmatically decided to alter the contents of his "recordings" to fit certain preconceptions he knew his audience to hold? If Johnny's recorded reality failed to conform to his audience's preconceptions of what that reality should be like, the audience would not pay him in whiskey for publishing his recordings.

Suppose Johnny's ruse worked, and his audience in the town bar took Johnny's apparent recordings but actual fictions as true and precise representations of reality, both because they conformed to and reinforced the audience's preconceived notions of what that reality should be and because Johnny had a knack for imitating voices and mannerisms astonishingly well? Given this ploy, Johnny would cease being merely a recording and reproducing device and become instead an artist involved in a complex dialogue with his audience and characters. If the townspeople of Loma were moved to action based upon the perceived "realism" of Johnny's fictions, and perhaps drove the Hawkins sisters out of the community the way

Americans drove Mexican workers out of the United States between 1931 and 1934, would Johnny Bear have any responsibility for such effects?

Is it true, as Steinbeck told Mavis McIntosh in 1935, that *In Dubious Battle* has "no author's moral point of view" (*SLL*, p. 105)? And is it the case, as has been suggested, and as Steinbeck seemed to want to believe, that this novel is "a scientific exploration of the stimulation and reaction of the mob"?[27]

Though Steinbeck appropriated a dramatic method popularized by such writers as William Dean Howells and Ivan Turgenev more than a century ago, a point of view that pretends to refine the author out of the picture, there can be no doubt that the author's moral point of view is present in every word and punctuation mark, not to mention every minute decision that goes into the construction of each work of art. Although this novel has often been labeled Steinbeck's most "objective" work, and in spite of the author's insistence upon his objectivity, it is obvious that *In Dubious Battle* is an intensely subjective novel. It reflects the very private and personal vision of John Steinbeck, a vision that has little if anything to do with the actual social/political/historical reality appropriated.

How scientific was this exploration? Obviously there is no science involved at all. Steinbeck was simply creating a fictional world in which the only exploration that takes place is within the author's mind. It would seem that Steinbeck, like many authors, did not know what he was really doing. He insisted alternately that his novel made no serious attempt at realism and that it was a scrupulously researched and accurate representation of reality. He insisted that there was no "author's moral point of view" and that he was "judging nothing, simply putting down the thing," when, in actuality, he seemed to be simply confusing his use of a dramatic method with true, and impossible, authorial objectivity.

In Dubious Battle is unmistakably a powerful and in many ways a brilliantly crafted work of fiction. As a vehicle it is superbly effective, and as a work of art it must be admired. And here the real irony of the novel arises. As Benson has pointed out, in spite of his protestations about accuracy, ultimately Steinbeck did not intend to write a journalistic account of a strike, and he did not intend for millions of readers around the world to accept his fiction as a mirror held up to proletarian reality. But he crafted so well and so convincingly that this is precisely what has happened. Ironically, a lesser artist—an artist such as Carlos Bulosan—could not make his journalistic account of the same phenomena prevail.

Today, agricultural labor in America is in desperate circumstances. Real income for migrant farm laborers in 1990 was estimated to be one-third to one-half of what it was twenty years before. With the recent influx of immigrants from countries such as Guatemala and Haiti, corporate agriculture is once again using the tactic that has worked for a century to repress labor costs. They use one ethnic group to undercut another. The estimated 800,000 migrant farm laborers in the nation are once again struggling to survive as they move from camp to camp. The impression one receives from this picture is that virtually nothing has changed since the 1930s.[28]

It is in some ways both indefensible and preposterous to wander around the elephants' graveyard of literary sources lamenting that an artist did not incorporate those sources exactly as we think they were. That is, of course, merely to wish that the artist had written a different book—the one we would like to write. However, at the risk of committing the unpardonable sin, in the end I cannot but wish Steinbeck had done precisely that—that he had left his phalanx theory in the tidal pool and written a novel that might have allowed America's outcast peoples their rightful voices, that might have helped, in Bulosan's words, "to blast the walls that imprisoned the American soul."

6

THOMAS M. TAMMARO

Sharing Creation

Steinbeck, *In Dubious Battle*, and the Working-Class Novel in American Literature

Peasant Song

When the sun rises, I go to work.
When the sun goes down, I take my rest.
I dig my well from which I drink.
I farm the soil which yields my food.
I share creation, Kings can do no more.

—Ancient Chinese song, 2500 B.C.

Virtually no modern working-class novels are included among those works traditionally found in undergraduate curricula in American literature. Furthermore, working-class novels are rarely, if ever, represented in the major anthologies that give each new generation of college students a sense of our national literature. Yet working-class literature surely deserves a place in our curricula.

"Proletarian literature," a generic name given to certain works produced mostly in the 1920s and 1930s, grew out of two suppositions: that human experience is influenced by the social, economic, and political environments, and that the best way to understand the phenomenon of the individual manipulated by forces beyond his or her control is through Marxist theory, which sees the dialectic between class and culture. Proletarian literature burst on the American scene during the 1920s and 1930s, a time when the social and political climates provided proletarian writers with ample grist for their literary mills. However, the mainstream critical literary consensus is that proletarian literature as a genre "dwindled away as a subject and a theory in the 1940s."[1]

Walter Rideout, in *The Radical Novel in the United States, 1900–1950*, which Frederick J. Hoffman calls the "best book on the subject" of proletarian literature,[2] defines the radical novel as "one which demonstrates, either explicitly or implicitly, that its author objects to human suffering imposed by some socioeconomic system and advocates that the system be fundamentally changed."[3] Hoffman believes that "almost invariably, radical is equivalent to proletarian, and especially in the American thirties."[4] Of Rideout's four types of radical novels, the "strike novel" is best represented by Steinbeck's *In Dubious Battle*, which Hoffman calls "the superior novel of this class."[5] As a type of literature, however, the label "proletarian" is too limited, being closely aligned to Marxist theory; the term "working-class" provides a broader perspective because the term is not so tightly tied to a specific political ideology or dogma.

In his excellent essay "Democratizing Literature: Issues in Teaching Working-Class Literature," Nicholas Coles offers a useful definition of working-class literature: "writing by working-class people—whether they are workers who write ('worker-writers') or professional writers from working-class backgrounds—that deals substantially with working-class life."[6] Coles continues:

> Writers who are also workers, while they write about much else besides work . . . have often sought in writing to explore the effects of the inescapable centrality of work in their lives: describing what they get out of work and what it takes out of them; perhaps asking how the conditions of work got this way and how they might be different. And in doing so, how they may encourage students who are or will be workers to do the same. In focusing on work itself, then, this literature illuminates a customary and perhaps necessary blindspot of much middle-class literature: it makes visible the human labor that invests everything we have and use.[7]

This definition is inclusive, free of ideological or doctrinaire ties. Perhaps one reason why working-class literature has not found its way into the canon is that the romance of modern American literature has not been with blue-collar workers and their lives and issues, but rather with the lives and issues of white-collar workers. And if the business of America is business, we understand, then, why so few working-class novels are represented in the American canon.

An understanding of the working-class experience in America is crucial to our understanding of the American experience. And it is especially crucial to our understanding of the reshaping of the American character in the last decades of the nineteenth century and the early decades of the twentieth as the country moved from an agrarian to an industrial culture and economy. With the rise of corporate America came the shifting concentration of wealth to fewer people (it is estimated that in 1892, 200,000 people owned 70 percent of the country's wealth). With the trend of concentrated wealth came the lowering of income for the masses. According to some estimates by the Brookings Institute, by the time of the crash of 1929 nearly 60 percent of American families lived below the poverty level. Coupled with new waves of immigrants entering the United States to take their places in the rank and files of industry, these explosive changes—changes that eminently revolve around the working-class—forever altered the fabric of American culture.

But why a vacuum in the literature of that experience? Why are those novels and that literature missing from the standard reading lists in our courses and not represented in our anthologies? Are there no writers, no novels, that speak to those issues? There are those who will be quick to say that Upton Sinclair's *The Jungle* is just such a book. Yet when *The Jungle* is read, taught, or represented in anthologies, it is often slighted, taught apologetically, or discussed or dismissed as an aberration, as second-rate, suggesting that working-class issues do not lend themselves to great art, for surely if they did, our *great* writers would have written about them. The implications of classism and elitism become embarrassingly apparent when such criticisms are put forth. When working-class literature is viewed, it is often viewed as merely communist, socialist, left-wing liberal propaganda written by individuals who were short on artistry but long on passion for reform and social conscience, for it is all too easy to remember Sinclair's pronouncement that he had come to Chicago's South Side "to write the *Uncle Tom's Cabin* of the labor movement."[8] Because the working-class experience is grossly underrepresented in American literature, verging, in fact, on near invisibility, the arguments used to justify the rightful placement of ethnic and women's literature in the American canon seem relevant in justifying the addition of working-class literature as well.

One reason for the absence of working-class literature in our curricula and canon is the failure to see the centrality of the working-class experience in American culture. More than anything else in our collective experience, it is our work that defines us. In fact, no other American institution embodies so many of the myths that feed the American psyche. How much of the American character has been nurtured by the myths of upward mobility, equal opportunity, a classless society, the land of opportunity, hard work and reward, pulling oneself up by one's own bootstraps, self-reliance, and rugged individualism? If these are the archetypal American democratic myths, then it is essential for our individual and collective psychological health to examine them carefully. Good working-class novels—and good working-class literature in general—can help us scrutinize these myths, for these are the myths that nurture young men and women in our culture as they train to take their places among the working ranks in America.

Steinbeck's *In Dubious Battle*—among the best of American working-class novels—can fill this vacuum and address this reluctance to read and study a literature that has too long been ignored and is central to our common experience. If Louis Owens is correct—and I think he is—that *In Dubious Battle* "is the most tightly knit of Steinbeck's work, illustrating a highly complex harmony between structure and materials," and that "it is perhaps his most artistically successful novel and a key work in the whole of his fiction,"[9] and if Warren French is correct—and I think he is also—that *In Dubious Battle* is the "best novel about a strike ever written because Steinbeck refused to become a blind partisan and rather showed how struggles between laborers and employers—however provoked and justified—can inevitably prove only destructive and demoralizing to both parties and also to society as a whole,"[10] then I believe we need to ask why this novel has not taken its place among the important and necessary works of American literature. With *In Dubious Battle* we have a novel about the nature of working-class issues that is rich in both artistry and depth.

Lack of artistry, excessive propaganda, and datedness—that too much time must be spent teaching social history instead of literary criticism—are charges frequently hurled against the teaching of working-class literature. In his essay "Aesthetics of the Proletarian Novel," Frederick J. Hoffman asserts that "the proletarian novels . . . of the Thirties now mainly exist as period pieces, to which one refers from time to time, but almost unbelievingly."[11] Critics have used these very charges to diminish and underscore the second-ratedness of *In Dubious Battle*. Hoffman thought *In Dubious Battle* "the superior novel of its class."[12] Yet even Hoffman—who obviously sees the artistry in Steinbeck's novel and the lack of it in other "strike novels" of proletarian literature—cannot bring himself to call Steinbeck a first-rate writer. He writes that "the fiction of Farrell, Steinbeck, and Dos Passos [survives] and this is largely because it was superior work, less given to formulas and more in the literary tradition of twentieth-century naturalism. None of these is a first-rate writer, but all of them offer a literature that resists the confinement of an ideological source and explanation."[13] Hoffman's curse-by-faint-praise criticism does underscore, however, the fact that *In Dubious Battle* transcends propaganda. More recently, Harold Bloom, in his cursory assessment of *In Dubious Battle* as "quite certainly a period piece . . . of more interest to social historians than to literary critics,"[14] failed to see beyond the dated charge.

Yet *In Dubious Battle* stands next to *The Grapes of Wrath* as one of Steinbeck's greatest artistic achievements. Its polemics and propaganda are negated by its objectivity—which has been discussed in detail by others—and by Steinbeck's failure to choose sides and create flat, unambiguous characters who woo our sympathies. Far from being polemical, *In Dubious Battle* succeeds because it *avoids* polemics and propaganda. Had Steinbeck wanted the novel to embrace polemics, to be a Communist book, all he would have needed to do was bring Doc Burton back into the struggle to take his place among the rank and file. Instead, he makes him disappear, and Doc becomes a kind of working man's "lone ranger" who appears when needed and then conveniently moves on—most likely to the next struggle—leaving behind a trail of good deeds and high philosophical concerns that transcend party line and ideology. Steinbeck's deliberate distancing of himself from Communist ideology in the novel was a stroke of aesthetic genius, placing him squarely on the side of writing informed by both personal vision and social conscience instead of writing informed *only* by social conscience.

Furthermore, the novel is not a period piece. It is not forever wedded to the plight of the agrarian working class of the 1930s, though that is certainly where the story emerges. On the contrary, one of the novel's strengths is that it is teachable and readable without a crash course in the social history of the 1930s. In many ways, one of the triumphs of *In Dubious Battle* is that its meaning and vision are not contingent upon time or place. Removed from its historical context, *In Dubious Battle* loses none of its richness and power. It still stands as the same hard-edged, face-to-face encounter with the human dilemma regarding the nature of work, power, personal freedom, and degree of responsibility and commitment individuals have toward their fellow human beings—all of this played out in a universe of benign indifference.

Other reasons account for the absence of working-class novels and literature in our course syllabi. For example, historically the relationship between organized labor and corporate America has been tenuous, to say the least. Relatedly, unionism has been equated with communism, more out of an anti-communist/anti-Soviet spirit than because of any real threat of communist subversion of the working classes. (Steinbeck cleverly deals with this issue in *In Dubious Battle* by showing how the workers' hunger has more to do with who they follow than their belief in any given ideology.) And the American xenophobic response to the flood of eastern European immigrants—especially during the early years of this century—and the strong ethnic presence in unions (and in working-class literature) certainly must be raised, especially as it is related to working-class issues.

Coles argues that "a preference [in literature] for the obscure and highly wrought, and a bias against the work of those who were not traditionally members of the trained literary elite: the literature of women, of black, of ethnic, and working-class writers . . . was excluded or admitted only by exception, in a form of discrimination that, at bottom, has less to do with valuations of literary quality than with the social distribution of power."[15]

Steinbeck knew he was going against the grain when he chose to write about Mexican-American field workers, *paisanos*, bindle stiffs, migrant workers, strikers, party organizers, and a host of other characters who move outside middle-class and mainstream life. And as Benson and Timmerman have documented, Steinbeck's knowledge of these people and their lives was not second- or third-hand knowledge, as critics have often accused, but rather first-hand knowledge, for as Benson states, "he knew them well from childhood on."[16,17]

In Dubious Battle brings many of the issues of working-class literature to the foreground, and it does so with finely tuned aesthetic and dramatic sensibilities. Coles writes that "engaging in a marginalized tradition such as working-class literature can put us in a position to learn again that there are other ways of reading, and texts that demand to be read in other ways. This discovery is especially important at a time when mostpeople [Cole is borrowing e. e. cummings's word] in all their diversity, go to college and take our literature courses."[18]

"For some students," Coles continues, "texts like these offer revelations of social worlds they had never imagined as existing; they respond like readers of documentary realism, with shock, concern, sometimes political questioning."[19] Thus, we allow our students to "share in creation" when we bring books such as *In Dubious Battle* into our classrooms and make them part of our tradition, because they are part of our tradition—and we can do this without sacrificing artistry and aesthetic excellence.

In Dubious Battle seems as relevant and useful a book in the 1990s as it was when it was published in 1936. We need only to look to the March 26, 1990, issue of *Time* magazine to see how near *In Dubious Battle* is to our times.

In the wake of the March 1990 strike by nine thousand Greyhound bus drivers against Greyhound Company, *Time* reported the results of its poll of American attitudes toward labor unions. While 73 percent of the people polled believed that the American worker still needed labor unions, 40 percent believed labor unions had too much power, while 33 percent believed they had just the right amount of power. Only a little more than one-fifth of those polled believed that unions did not have enough power.

While many believe the death knell of the modern labor movement was rung by Ronald Reagan's decision to fire Professional Air Traffic Controllers Organization strikers in 1981 and replace them with nonunion workers, others point to the general decline of unionism since the end of World War II. According to *Time*, union membership in 1945, for example, "made up more than 35% of the non-agricultural work force; by 1980, they had dropped to 22%, and have fallen considerably since."[20] To many, the Reagan years are seen as a time of "open season on unions," and they point to a number of government, private, and public actions that have generally weakened unionism. Many union loyalists believe that too often labor disputes are more about getting rid of unions than they are about wages and fair labor practices.

Working-class literature may be invisible because Americans do not think of work and working as "an art." Instead, work is seen in terms of product and production, a commodity to be consumed and devoured, something to nourish the material body (i.e., we work for our "bread and butter"; we go to the "salt mines"; we "bring home the bacon"; we measure our collective work as a "gross national product"). It is an attitude based upon a materialistic paradigm, not an imaginative or creative one. We work to have "something to put our hands on," to echo Ben's gauge of success in *Death of a Salesman*, Arthur Miller's play about work. That which is made material and concrete in our language is made invisible in our literary canon because it is so much a part of our devalued daily experience. And so we "take vacations from," make temporarily invisible, that which reminds us of our daily struggle to survive.

As a working-class novel, *In Dubious Battle* remains as strong and central a work of literature as ever. Read against today's headlines, it is difficult to dismiss it as a period piece. The issues of labor, work, management—all of which are addressed and explored in *In Dubious Battle*—still remain with us, unresolved, uncertain, and underrepresented in our national literature.

7

THOMAS FENSCH

Reflections of Doc
The Persona of Ed Ricketts in *Of Mice and Men*

Like a compass, which will always turn and point to magnetic north, Steinbeck turns to and uses the personalities of friends and acquaintances in his fiction. Steinbeck expert and librarian Pauline Pearson once said to me, "There is an Ed Ricketts character in all of Steinbeck's books." I have thought about that statement for some months. Recently I was able to talk again with Pearson. "If you look hard enough, you will always find an Ed Ricketts character in Steinbeck's books," she asserted again. "There is an Ed Ricketts character in at least five of John's books: *In Dubious Battle, The Moon Is Down, Cannery Row,* and *Sweet Thursday,* and I think there is a considerable amount of Ed Ricketts in the character Lee in *East of Eden.*"[1] Anyone who seriously claims to know Steinbeck should know Ricketts. But is Pearson correct? Does Ed "Doc" Ricketts appear in book after book by Steinbeck?

Richard Astro, writing about Ricketts in *John Steinbeck and Edward F. Ricketts: The Shaping of a Novelist,* says Ricketts appears in at least six Steinbeck books. "Ed Ricketts serves in various degrees as the source of Steinbeck's personae in six novels and novelettes (*In Dubious Battle, The Grapes of Wrath, The Moon Is Down, Cannery Row, Burning Bright, Sweet Thursday*), and in one short story ('The Snake'). No analysis of Steinbeck's world view, his philosophy of life, can proceed without a careful study of the life, work, and ideas of this remarkable human being who was Steinbeck's closest personal and intellectual companion for nearly two decades."[2]

Ricketts appears as Doc Burton in *In Dubious Battle*. His ideas are a part of the character, philosophy, and speech of Jim Casy in *The Grapes of Wrath*. He is Dr. Winter in *The Moon Is Down*, Doc in *Cannery Row* and *Sweet Thursday*, Friend Ed in *Burning Bright*, and Doc Phillips in "The Snake." Ricketts is also the subject of Steinbeck's classic memoir/biography/obituary, "About Ed Ricketts," in *The Log from the Sea of Cortez*, perhaps the most widely known memoir in twentieth-century American literature. Of these various fictional versions of the Ricketts personality, Astro comments that Doc Burton in *In Dubious Battle* was "in fact modeled directly on Ed Ricketts."[3] Doc Winter was a "loosely fictionalized version of Ed Ricketts."[4] And "surely Joe Saul [in *Burning Bright*] is John Steinbeck and Friend Ed is Ed Ricketts."[5] Of the woman who watched the snake in the short story "The Snake," Astro affirms that it really happened as Steinbeck told it, in Ed Ricketts's Cannery Row lab. And, of course, Doc Phillips was Ricketts.[6]

Since Ed Ricketts appears, as Pearson and Astro state, in a variety of Steinbeck books, is there an Ed Ricketts character in *Of Mice and Men*? At first glance, the answer appears to be no. The novelette is taut and lean—stylistically one of Steinbeck's best. I compare it to Hemingway's *The Old Man and the Sea*; both are short novels with scarcely a word wasted in either. George and Lennie are clearly individuals with distinct personalities; however, neither appears to possess much of the personality or philosophy of Ed Ricketts. Steinbeck presents them to us in a remarkable way not duplicated in his other books. His use of the *middle distance* is one of the keys to *Of Mice and Men*; as T. K. Whipple claims, "Steinbeck places his characters not too close nor too far away," so that "we can see their performances with greatest clarity and fullness."[7] Neither George nor Lennie appears to have much in common with Ed Ricketts, but does any other character in *Of Mice and Men* reflect Steinbeck's view of Ricketts?

The answer is that Ed Ricketts appears in *Of Mice and Men* as both a single character *and through Ricketts's point of view*. In the middle of the book, we see him in the character Slim, the "jerkline driver":

> A tall man stood in the doorway. He held a crushed Stetson hat under his arm while he combed his long, black, damp hair straight back. Like others he wore blue jeans and a short denim jacket. When he finished combing his hair he moved into the room, and he moved with a majesty only achieved by royalty and master craftsmen. He was a jerkline skinner, the prince of the ranch, capable of killing a fly on the wheeler's butt with a bull whip without touching the mule. There was a gravity in his manner and a quiet so profound that all talk stopped when he spoke. His authority was so great that his word was taken on any subject, be it politics or love. This was Slim, the jerkline skinner. His hatchet face was ageless. He might have been thirty-five or fifty. His ear heard more than was said to him, and his slow speech had overtones not of thought, but of understanding beyond thought. His hands, large and lean, were as delicate in their action as those of a temple dancer.[8]

Slim is presented not only as a wise, almost godlike figure, but also as the only character who bridges the gap between George and Lennie and the rest of the ranch. He stands up to Curley, he referees the episode when Carlson urges Candy to kill his old dog, he gives a pup to Lennie to keep, and ultimately he is the fulcrum for the final action of the book.

But there is more to Ed Ricketts's involvement in *Of Mice and Men*; both Steinbeck's middle distance stance throughout the novelette and his nonjudgmental point of view reflect Ricketts's philosophy. And this philosophy dominates *Of Mice and Men* more, perhaps, than it does any other book by Steinbeck. Astro writes:

> Viewed in perspective, what Steinbeck seems to be doing in *Of Mice and Men* is using Ricketts's ideas about non-teleological thinking not as theme, but as fictional method. He tells the story of Lennie and George from a non-blaming point of view, but never does he suggest the unimportance of the teleological considerations symbolized by Lennie's dream (of a farm of his own). Actually, Steinbeck's method in *Of Mice and Men* emerges through the consciousness of Slim, the jerkline skinner and "prince of the ranch," who moves "with majesty only achieved by royalty and master craftsmen." It is Slim, a character whose "ear heard more than was said to him" and whose "slow speech had overtones not of thought, but understanding beyond thought," who understands George and Lennie's land hunger but who also knows the dream will fail. And it is Slim who affirms the need for direct, purposive action by George after Lennie kills Curley's wife.[9]

The nonjudgmental ideas of Ed Ricketts are also reflected in the novelette's original title: *Something That Happened*.

In his monumental biography of Steinbeck, *The True Adventures of John Steinbeck, Writer*, Jackson J. Benson observes:

In an extension of his previous effort, in *In Dubious Battle*, to present a conflict without taking sides, another experiment had to do with the attempt to write from a completely non-te-leological standpoint: no cause and no effect, no problems and solutions, no heroes and villains—just as he calls his first manuscript "Something That Happened." In this effort he was no doubt encouraged by his association with Ricketts, which had become extremely close both during the summer before his trip to Mexico and during the months that followed.[10]

Thus we see Ricketts reflected in both *character* and *method* in the novel.

Astro also suggests that "the novelist's use of Ricketts's *modus operandi* in *Of Mice and Men* enabled him to avoid pretentious philosophizing while recording his beliefs. And in telling his story about the fractured dreams of mice and men with a precision and lucidity unexcelled in any of his other works, Steinbeck testifies to the fact that Ed Ricketts not only helped teach him how to 'live into life,' but that [Ricketts] also had a hand in helping [Steinbeck] to record his observations of it."[11]

Thus, I believe we can safely add *Of Mice and Men* to the list of books in which Ed Ricketts has a fictional but significant role. *Of Mice and Men* is the seventh book of John Steinbeck's in which his friend (Friend Ed in *Burning Bright*) plays a major role as character. In *Of Mice and Men*, Ricketts's philosophy also contributes to the enduring qualities that make the story of Lennie and George so memorable.

8

ROBERT E. MORSBERGER

Tell Again, George

Many novelists have also been playwrights or have adapted their fiction to the stage, with various degrees of success, and a few writers have turned their plays into novels, but beginning with *Of Mice and Men* and continuing with *The Moon Is Down* and *Burning Bright*, John Steinbeck claimed to have invented what he called "a new form—the play-novelette."[1] What is unique about Steinbeck's play-novelettes is that he conceived them simultaneously in both forms.

In his introduction to the Bantam edition of *Burning Bright*, Steinbeck explained the rationale by which he undertook his three play-novelettes. He claimed that he found it difficult to read plays; furthermore, only a limited number of theatergoers might see even a successful play. He considered that the novelette version would find a larger audience. He also wanted to provide the director, producer, and performers with more descriptive and interpretive detail than the terse stage directions in an acting copy of a play. The novelette, he thought, provided more fully the author's intention.[2] Conversely, the discipline of the theater forces the novelist to be clear and concise. Despite the downward curve of his success with the play-novelette, Steinbeck found the combination "highly re-warding. It gives a play a wide chance of being read and a piece of fiction a chance of being played without the usual revision."[3]

Of Mice and Men was published as a novel before Steinbeck dramatized it, but apparently he wrote it in such a way that it could easily be turned into a play; in 1936, while the work was in progress, he wrote to George Albee, "It is a tricky little thing designed to teach me to write for the theatre."[4] At this time, Steinbeck had had comparatively little exposure to the stage and to theater people, but in his best work, he wrote some of the best working-class dialogue in American literature, and episodes from some of his novels read almost like scenes from a play. (It is worth noting here that a great deal of the dialogue in Nunnally Johnson's screenplay of *The Grapes of Wrath* and in the currently successful stage version by the Steppenwolf Theatre Company of Chicago, which won the Tony Award as best play of 1989, comes verbatim from the novel. "The play's language is that of the author," said adapter Frank Galati. "[T]here may be five or six lines in the play that are not from the novel, but that's it."[5])

Before he could do his own adaptation of *Of Mice and Men*, Steinbeck agreed to let the Theatre Union, a labor drama group in San Francisco, stage its own version to open its new Green Street Theatre in North Beach. When its president, Wellman Farley, told Steinbeck he wanted to put on plays about local history, Steinbeck presented him with a manuscript of the not-yet-published novel.[6] The Theatre Union dramatization opened on May 21 and ran on Friday and Saturday nights for sixteen performances.[7] John Hobart, reviewing it in the *San Francisco Chronicle*, found that it "follows the novel closely; the dialogue has been lifted straight from the book and trans-ferred to the stage with hardly a single change."[8] Although in his introduction to *Burning Bright*, thirteen years later, Steinbeck claimed that his short novels "can be played simply by lifting out the dialogue,"[9] Hobart found that "since Steinbeck was writing primarily for readers, the result is a play that seems slightly ill at ease in the theatre."[10] Likewise, Margaret Shedd found that the Theatre Union version "does no more than black in the tantalizing outlines, with too much sentimental detail of rabbits and murders and with gaping omissions."[11] In this form, she concluded, "*Of Mice and Men* is certainly not a great play, although, just as certainly it has in it the raw material of one."[12] Steinbeck himself conceded that when he undertook his own dramatization for experienced theater people, he had to do extensive rewriting.[13]

Of Mice and Men attracted several playwrights, but Annie Laurie Williams, of Steinbeck's agents McIntosh and Otis, recommended the novel to Beatrice Kaufman, wife of playwright George S. Kaufman, and she wrote enthusiastically to Steinbeck that the novel "drops almost naturally into play form and no one knows that better than you."[14] Though his own plays had been chiefly comedies, usually in collaboration with Moss Hart, Kaufman was eager to direct *Of Mice and Men* and encouraged Steinbeck to dramatize his novel. When Steinbeck showed his adaptation to Kaufman, the veteran playwright knew it needed work and took Steinbeck to his farm in Bucks County, Pennsylvania, where for an intense week the novelist revised the script under Kaufman's guidance.[15] "It is only the second act that seems to me to need fresh invention," Kaufman said. "You have the two natural scenes for it—the bunkhouse and the Negro's room, but I think the girl should come into both these scenes, and that the fight between Lennie and Curley, which will climax Act Two, must be over the girl. I think the girl should have a scene with

Lennie before the scene in which he kills her. The girl, I think, should be drawn more fully; she is the motivating force of the whole thing and should loom larger."[16]

Steinbeck followed these suggestions in revising his script. The dialogue in act 1 follows the first two chapters of the novel almost verbatim; even the stage directions are usually verbatim from the novel's descriptive and narrative details. Of necessity, Steinbeck had to omit some descriptive passages that could not be staged, particularly the novel's opening four pages and the sentimental description of Slim. Of course, the language lifted from the novel for stage directions and character descriptions would not be heard by the audience, but reading the opening scenes is essentially the same experience as reading the first two chapters. However, on her first appearance, in the second scene, Curley's wife gets a bit more dialogue in the play: "I'm just lookin' for somebody to talk to. Don't you never jus' want to talk to somebody?"[17] The addition of just these two sentences makes her a bit more sympathetic. After she leaves, her perfume lingers. "God Almighty, did you smell that stink she's got on?" George asks. "I can still smell her. Don't have to see her to know she's around."[18] Thus, in the next scene, before the fight with Lennie, Steinbeck adds the detail of having Curley sniff her perfume and swear she was there.

Again, in act 2, scene 1, just before Curley's appearance and the fight, Curley's wife has three additional speeches that help make her sympathetic, more a victim than a provocateur. In the novel, she does not appear in this scene at all. In the play, after agreeing to include Candy as a partner in the farm, George adds the line, "You know, seems to me I can almost smell that carnation stuff that god-damn tart dumps on herself." Here Curley's wife enters and says angrily, "Who you callin' a tart! I come from a nice home. I was brung up by nice people. Nobody never got to me before I was married. I was straight. I tell you. I was good. (A little plaintively.) I was. (Angrily again) You know Curley. You know he wouldn't stay with me if he wasn't sure. . . . You got no right to call me a tart." When George responds by asking her why she is always hanging around guys when she has a husband, she replies, pleadingly, "Sure I got a man. He ain't never home. I got nobody to talk to. I got nobody to be with. Think I can just sit home and cook for Curley? I want to see somebody. Just see 'em an' talk to 'em. There ain't no women. I can't walk to town. And Curley don't take me to no dances now. I tell you I jus' want to talk to somebody." When George replies by asking why she gives him the eye, she answers sadly, "I just wanta be nice."[19] Then, hearing Curley and Slim approach, she disappears.

Considering the impact she makes, it is surprising how brief a role Curley's wife has in the novel. Before the chapter when Lennie kills her, she has only two brief appearances, one for two pages, another for nine. In chapter 5, she has 10 more pages, for a total of 21 pages out of 186. Probably the role seems larger because Curley and the others frequently talk about her. But in the play and film versions, the enlarged role earns the actress supporting star billing. Again, further changes make her more sympathetic in the play. When she interrupts Candy, Crooks, and Lennie in Crooks's room, in the novel she threatens to have Crooks lynched by lying that he made advances to her. The play cuts this unsympathetic passage and, instead, has George come into the scene and argue with her. At the end, as she is about to leave, she speaks to Lennie with "a note of affection in her voice" as she realizes that it was he who ruined her husband's hand. She says to him,

"Well . . . maybe you're dumb like they say . . . an' maybe . . . you're the only guy on the ranch with guts. (She puts her hand on Lennie's shoulder. He looks up in her face and a smile grows on his face. She strokes his shoulder.) You're a nice fella."[20] This, of course, leads more naturally to the brief intimacy between them in the barn.

In the barn scene, the play adds another detail, bringing her there more plausibly by having her hide with a packed suitcase, prepared to run away. Thus, when she tells Lennie about her dream of becoming a movie star, the novel's "I coulda" is changed to "I'm gonna," and her unexpected death at the moment of her supposed liberation becomes even more poignant. The final scene of the play cuts several passages from the novel; it omits Lennie's fantasy conversations with Aunt Clara and with a gigantic rabbit, and it ends with the gunshot that kills Lennie, dropping the subsequent anticlimactic dialogue when the lynch mob and Slim reappear.

These changes, plus a few other minor ones, tighten the dramatic structure and impact of the work. When he received the New York Drama Critics' Circle Award for the play, Steinbeck modestly said that Kaufman deserved most of the credit, but all the dialogue is Steinbeck's, and at least 80 percent of it comes verbatim from the novel. Kaufman deserves credit for advising Steinbeck to enlarge the role of Curley's wife; it is not clear which of them decided to make her more sympathetic.

Otherwise, Kaufman's chief contribution was as director. He considered Victor McLaglen for the crucial role of Lennie but decided it might be better not to have to put up with star temperament, even though stars' names were helpful at the box office.[21] Accordingly, he cast Wallace Ford and Broderick Crawford, then comparative unknowns, as George and Lennie. Will Geer played Slim, and Claire Luce was Curley's wife.

Before rehearsals started, Steinbeck met with the staff, said that everything seemed to be in such good hands that he was not needed, and departed for California. Much to Kaufman's chagrin, Steinbeck was in Los Gatos when the play opened in New York on November 23, 1937, at the Music Box.[22] He kept in touch by phone, however, and was gratified to learn that the reviews ranged from enthusiastic to ecstatic. Brooks Atkinson called *Mice* "a masterpiece of the New York stage."[23] Recalling that Steinbeck was known to have written the novel "with the stage in mind," Atkinson found that "the economy of the story, the unity of the mood, the simple force of the characters, the tang of the dialogue are compactly dramatic, and *Of Mice and Men* is not theatre second hand. . . . To be technical about it, *Of Mice and Men* is a perfect work of art."[24] It ran for 207 performances in New York and beat *Our Town* by a vote of twelve to four for the New York Drama Critics' Circle Award as best play of the year. In presenting the award, the critics praised the play "for its direct force and perception in handling a theme genuinely rooted in American life."[25] Later, more hostile critics would accuse Steinbeck of sentimentality, but in 1937, what impressed critics was, in George Jean Nathan's words, the play's "unabashed realism," its "beautifully honest . . . scrutiny of speech, act, emotion, and character."[26] Indeed, the realism in both action and language then seemed so raw that some viewers left the theater in indignation, and *Of Mice and Men* has never since ceased to be attacked by puritanical and right-wing censors.

In April 1939, a London production, with John Mills and Niall MacGinnis as George and Lennie, opened for a successful run. Reviewer Charles Morgan particularly praised the performance of Mills, "who, with a thousand unemphatic touches, none of them deliberately explanatory, used Mr. Steinbeck's dialogue to build up a portrait of a lovable man who probably believed himself to be a tough realist but who . . . was at heart a dreamer of boyish dreams. The part is so truly written and so faithfully performed that when, at the end, George shoots his friend Lennie, deliberately, hopelessly, and because he still loves him, what might have been a falsely symbolic or an arbitrarily melodramatic ending is neither of these things but falls into place as natural and inevitable."[27]

In 1958, Ira J. Bilowit and Wilson Lehr adapted *Of Mice and Men* into a musical play, with lyrics by Bilowit and music by Alfred Brooks. It played briefly off Broadway but fared poorly. Louis Calta judged that while "Mr. Steinbeck's drama still remains a work of substance and power," the score and lyrics "never quite became an integral part of the drama," lacked "the necessary passion, grandeur and breadth," and "at no time . . . heighten the intensity of Mr. Steinbeck's prize-winning play."[28] An operatic version by Carlisle Floyd fared no better in 1970; when it was revived in San Francisco in 1974, music critic Martin Bernheimer judged that the simple eloquence of Steinbeck's language sounds "stilted, silly and artificial when blown up for grand operatic treatment."[29]

In 1938 Nathan predicted that the play could never be filmed, that the movies would never "dare to risk such things intact," since its language and subject matter would get it shot down by the Hays office and would "bring down the wrath of every women's club in the land."[30] Meanwhile, Steinbeck had been associating with documentary film director Pare Lorentz on several abortive documentary films. Lorentz led Steinbeck to director Lewis Milestone, who was eager to film *Of Mice and Men*. Mervyn LeRoy, who had directed such hard-hitting films as *Little Caesar* (1930), *I Am a Fugitive from a Chain Gang* (1932), and *They Won't Forget* (1937), had also expressed interest, but Steinbeck was disgusted when LeRoy wanted to rewrite the story to have Lennie merely accused of killing Curley's wife. LeRoy argued that this would keep sympathy for Lennie, overlooking the fact that it would destroy the dramatic and symbolic structure and the climax of Steinbeck's work.[31] By contrast, Milestone, whose credits included *All Quiet on the Western Front* (1930), was noted for making faithful adaptations of literary works. As he observed, "Throughout my career I've tried not so much to express a philosophy as to restate in filmic terms my agreement with whatever the author of a story I like is trying to say." He also said, "My approach, my style is governed by the story, not the story by my style."[32] Having read the novel and seen the play, Milestone resolved to do justice to them and made the film as a labor of love, on a miniscule budget, for producer Hal Roach (formerly noted for Laurel and Hardy comedies) under the banner of United Artists. Both Milestone and screenwriter Eugene Solow were so devoted to the project that they wrote the entire script on speculation, risking their own time and money.

Solow's screenplay removed some of Steinbeck's then-censurable language but kept his virile vernacular and supplemented the play with some details from the novel. Actually, "hell" and "son-of-a-bitch" are the only profanity Steinbeck used, but a journalist had once referred to *Mice*'s "two-syllable language as mean, hard, and sometimes as foul as their [the characters'] semi-savage existence."

Milestone, a cousin of violinist Nathan Milstein, wanted a distinguished score and persuaded Aaron Copland to write his first music for a Hollywood film (Copland had previously scored a documentary movie). Copland had read the novel but insisted on rereading it before accepting the assignment to make sure it would suit his creative powers. Convinced that it did, he cabled his acceptance and within twenty-four hours was on his way west. "Here," he said, "was an American theme, by a great American writer, demanding appropriate music."[33] Running the unscored film back and forth, Copland said, "I was genuinely moved by *Of Mice and Men* and by the inspired performances, and I found that the scenes induced the music if I turned to them while composing."[34]

Ordinarily, composers were given only two weeks to produce a film score, but Copland insisted upon six for *Of Mice and Men*, and, unlike many film composers, who use arrangers, he did his own orchestration.[35] Instead of calling attention to itself, Copland's restrained music underscores and intensifies the action in such episodes as the threshing machine and the fight between Curley and Lennie, climaxed, when Lennie crushes Curley's hand, by a grinding dissonant chord that David Diamond called "extraordinary." Diamond added, "This is what film music's all about."[36] "After all," Copland wrote, "film music makes sense only if it helps the film; no matter how good, distinguished or successful, the music must be secondary in importance to the story being told on the screen."[37] Avoiding full-blown symphonic music, he used "more natural sounding instrumentation—solo flute, flutes together, and a guitar for a campfire scene."[38] At times, he tried to provide the sort of tunes the farmhands might have whistled. "The temper of the music varied with every scene," he recalled, "but always I tried to keep away from the overlush harmonies that are so common on the screen and usually defeat their own purpose by overemphasis."[39]

After the success of his score for *Of Mice and Men*, Copland went on to score films of several American literary classics— *Our Town, Washington Square* (filmed as *The Heiress*, for which he won an Academy Award), and *The Red Pony*, the concert suite from which is one of Copland's finest works. In 1942, Copland composed *Music for Movies,* a suite for small orchestra that was derived but not transcribed literally from his scores for *Of Mice and Men, Our Town,* and the documentary *The City.* Two of its five movements come from *Of Mice and Men.*

The cast had no established stars. Spencer Tracy, James Cagney, and John Garfield were all eager to play George but were prevented by other commitments as well as by the fact that Milestone probably could not have afforded them. None of the stage players was retained. Milestone cast Burgess Meredith (who had made only one previous film—*Winterset* [1936])—as George. Lennie was played by Lon Chaney, Jr., in his first starring role. Possibly, Chaney's hulking presence as a half-wit did as much as his father's reputation to trap him later in horror movie roles, but his performance was a sympathetic one, revealing a remarkable sensitivity one would not expect from viewing him subsequently as the wolf man, the mummy, or the Frankenstein monster. Betty Field, an unknown, replaced Claire Luce as Curley's wife, who has no name in the novel or play but is called Mae in the film. Curley was Bob Steele, formerly seen only in B-class westerns, and Charles Bickford was a stalwart Slim. Leigh Whipper, as Crooks, had one of the most dignified and eloquent roles the screen had so far provided for a black performer.

Completed in forty-two days for under $300,000, *Of Mice and Men* was called "the most economical Grade A movie to come out of Hollywood in a decade."[40] Milestone had wanted to shoot the exteriors at the actual ranch in the Salinas Valley that Steinbeck had used as a model, but finding the ranch house hopelessly run-down, he had a replica built on the Agoura Ranch of William Randolph Hearst, which was rented for a nominal twenty-five dollars a day. One great advantage the film has over the play or the novel is Norbert Brodine's photography. Brodine succeeds in visualizing the hills and fields of California, the actual farm work, and the lives of the hands in the mess room and bunkhouse, thus conveying the migrants' loneliness and love of the land and providing a much more extensive visual record of the agrarian 1930s than the film of *The Grapes of Wrath*, which shows very little of actual farm life. Otis Ferguson, reviewing the film for the *New Republic*, thought the movie more fluid than either the play or the novel, finding it "in many visual qualities more actual and vivid."

The movie opens with the then-innovative device of beginning the action before the title and credits. We first see Lennie and George running from an armed posse and escaping by hopping on a passing freight train, after which we read the title and credits chalked on the side of passing boxcars. In this way the theme of fear and flight is immediately established, and the opening scene balances the ending. Next comes the evening campsite by the Salinas River. Perhaps to keep squeamish viewers from being startled, the film substitutes a dead bird for Lennie's dead mouse, thus losing half the point of the title. To demonstrate his strength, Lennie lifts a loaded grain wagon with Slim sitting on it and George hanging on the wheel, a contrived implausibility perhaps borrowed from *Les Miserables*, but which also has a folk quality as a legendary feat of strength. As Curley, Steele is small and vicious, but he wears black leather gloves on both hands, thus coming across as a dirty boxer rather than an insecure husband who wears one Vaseline-filled glove on his left hand to keep it soft for his bride. Thus, when Lennie crushes that hand, the impact is lessened.

Despite these flaws, the movie *Of Mice and Men* is a closer and more complete version of the book than any other film of a major Steinbeck novel. Brilliant though *The Grapes of Wrath* is on screen, it evades some of the novel's more explicit social and political details and condenses Steinbeck's epic. Done on a smaller scale, *Of Mice and Men* benefits from a tight unity and a stronger story line that achieves an archetypal folk quality in its dramatization of American loneliness, self-destructive innocence, and the dream of a place of one's own, elements that are more universal and timeless than the outrages inflicted on the Okies. People are still dreaming the same dreams as Lennie and George and are still being hurt by them.

The first of Steinbeck's novels to be filmed, *Of Mice and Men* premiered on December 22, 1939, just a few weeks before *The Grapes of Wrath*, to almost universal critical acclaim, but because 1939 and 1940 provided more outstanding movies than any in Hollywood history, *Mice* was edged out by blockbuster films with stellar casts—*Gone with the Wind, Jesse James, Mr. Smith Goes to Washington, Dodge City*, and *Dark Victory*—and fared poorly at the box office. And although it has become a critical cliché to accuse Steinbeck of sentimentalism, in 1939 and 1940, *Of Mice and Men* was called too "grim and uncompromising," without enough escapist fare. Accordingly, advertising was shifted to emphasize sex, by featuring sensual poses of Betty Field with the captions, "Unwanted, she fought for the one thing that is every woman's birthright," and "A thrilling drama of careless love."[41] This campaign deservedly failed, but in time the picture finally took its place as an enduring classic.

Curiously, it has not been released on videotape, so the only film versions currently available for home consumption are the NBC production that was telecast in color on November

29, 1981, and the 1982 film version. An earlier TV version, a Previews IV production starring George Segal as George and Nicol Williamson as Lennie, which was aired in 1968, is not on tape and is questionable for suggesting a homosexual relationship between George and Lennie that is emphatically not in Steinbeck's novel or play. George and Lennie's unusually close relationship, which they as well as other migrants comment on, is not due to homoeroticism but to the fact that George feels responsible for Lennie, whom he calls his cousin, and who would be helpless without him. Without Lennie to get him into trouble and be a pain in the neck, George thinks he could be a carefree loner, but he needs Lennie to provide a sense of family and to keep alive the dream of a place of their own. Lennie's death need not keep George, Candy, and Crooks from pooling their resources to buy the farm, but with Lennie gone, the dream dies, and they all know it.

The NBC version has a lot to recommend it, including first-rate performances. Robert Blake, who also was executive producer, gives a solid performance as George, possibly truer than Meredith's in the 1939 film. Fine though he was, Meredith was possibly too clever, ingratiating, even a bit cute as George. By contrast, Blake is a thoroughly believable no-nonsense working man who smiles only when revealing his affection for Lennie. As Lennie, Randy Quaid is more excitable and expressive in both face and voice than the rather impassive Chaney. When finally Quaid's Lennie "sees" the farm with rabbits just before George shoots him, we realize that the resting place across the river is heaven, not an earthly habitation. Blake and Quaid play against each other admirably, giving performances as valid as those of Meredith and Chaney in the classic film. The supporting cast members do equally well. Pat Hingle plays the boss as a heavy-set, phlegmatic, authoritarian type, and

Ted Neeley is exceedingly nasty as Curley, a diminutive dandy who preens himself as he struts or rides about dressed in black like a nineteenth-century gunfighter. As his wife (called Mae, as she is in the 1939 film), Cassie Yates is a frustrated rural slattern with a tense, drawn look that suggests she will not keep her beauty long and will soon become just another gaunt, haggard farm wife. We first see her playing with a puppy in the barn; inevitably, her coming back to get that puppy will lead to her encounter with Lennie and to her death. In her cheap, tight cotton dresses, she is more victim than vamp, and her looking for people to talk to is not erotic but simply an attempt to find company to ease the loneliness caused by a sadistic husband who pays attention to her only when he is jealous. As Yates plays her, Mae is sour-faced and innocent. A scene in which father and son slurp pie and guzzle milk like a pair of hogs at the trough while Mae looks on in distaste reveals her dilemma without a word of dialogue.

The bunkhouse scenes have a gritty realism, and the cast seems thoroughly at home there. Mitch Ryan is a stalwart Slim, and Whitman Mayo brings dignity to his role as Crooks, the black outcast. Especially memorable is Lew Ayres as Candy, the one-handed swamper. White-haired, balding, grizzled, and stubble-bearded, Ayres is aged beyond recognition from his roles as the boyish soldier in *All Quiet on the Western Front*, the drunken playboy in *Holiday*, and the young Dr. Kildare. He has so immersed himself in the role that he seems to have become the old derelict. His grief over the killing of his old dog, his eager hope as he joins George and Lennie in their dream, and his plaintive sense of loss when the dream is destroyed are profoundly affecting. In some ways, his performance is the most brilliant of the production.

The script, by E. Nick Alexander, is based on Solow's screenplay for the 1939 film, which in turn takes most of its language directly from Steinbeck. Alexander adds an episode in which George and Lennie escape from a mounted posse by hiding in a field with corn high enough to conceal them from pursuit, followed by a scene in which the fugitives go to Lennie's Aunt Clara (who is dead in the novel and play), who here shelters and feeds them and listens to George's complaints about how Lennie keeps spoiling his chances for a good life. She reminds him that he has no obligation to Lennie and can abandon him at any time. Attempting to do so, George tells Lennie to wait on the porch until he calls and then hitches a ride on a truck heading out of town. But after about half a mile, he jumps off and returns for Lennie, just in time, as it turns out, for the posse has reappeared, and the two migrants must flee again. This time they race through a woods, cross a stream, and find refuge at the pool where Steinbeck's work opens.

At the pool, George sees Lennie playing with a dead mouse, which is indeed a mouse this time, not a bird, as it was in the 1939 film. The farm sequences open with a close-up of a pocket watch being snapped shut as the boss looks through a window to see George and Lennie, late, approaching the house. Thus tension is immediately established. The farm itself looks absolutely authentic, right down to the outhouses. Since California is now too congested, director Reza Badiyi took his company on location to Texas, which, aside from looking too flat, offers a lush setting for the farm near Soledad. The many scenes of farm life are filmed with a lyricism that counterpoints the human tragedy.

The main weakness of the 1981 production is the score by George Romanis, which is too often loud, obtrusive, and unsubtle, providing literal transcriptions of folk songs such as "Skip to My Lou," "Turkey in the Straw," the inevitable

"Red River Valley," and others. A plaintive rendition of "Shenandoah" accompanies Candy's expression of loneliness and his desire to join George and Lennie. After the murder, we hear "Red River Valley" again, rendered in a funereal manner, and at the end, as George walks alone down a road, carrying his bindle, we hear "Going Home" from the *Largo* movement of Dvorak's *New World Symphony*. This is not the last shot, however, for during the end credits, we see George and Lennie, timelessly together, walking through a waist-high field of waving wheat. The score is too obvious. Instead of writing original music in a folk idiom, like Aaron Copland, Romanis simply gives us traditional folk songs, nudging us with corn-ball cues that distract from the dialogue and asking us to accept their use as profound. Despite the music and a few flaws in the script, however, the 1981 TV version is commendable and is the best one readily available unless the 1939 film is released on videotape.

In 1992 a new large-screen movie version of *Of Mice and Men* was released by MGM to respectful but not enthusiastic reviews. Under the direction of Gary Sinise, Sinise and John Malkovich re-create their roles as George and Lennie from the 1980 Steppenwolf Theatre production. Sinise, who also played Tom Joad in the Steppenwolf stage version of *The Grapes of Wrath*, has a dedication to Steinbeck and credits a high school field trip to a production of *Of Mice and Men* at the Guthrie Theatre in Minneapolis with turning him on to literature and making him determined to become an actor.[42] Impressed with his work in the Broadway run of *The Grapes of Wrath*, Elaine Steinbeck gave him permission to film *Mice*. Sinise says he saw the film in his head before he began to make it, but though he opened it up visually, to keep it from seeming claustrophobic and talky, he retained what he calls "the purity of the story's heartbreaking tragedy," which "is dramatic enough in its own right. I didn't want to juice it up with a lot of sex, violence, montage techniques, or too much score."[43] Sinise avoided the 1981 television version's flaw of having too obtrusive a musical background. He observed that "there are a lot of moments in the story that just cry out for scoring; more *sad* music here, more *crisis* music there. Somebody else would have scored this thing to the hilt."[44] Mark Isham's unobtrusive music is effective and Coplandesque but unmemorable.

Visually, Sinise's is the most striking of all the film versions. Beautifully photographed by Kenneth MacMillan, it was shot on locations around Santa Ynez that look absolutely right, with the ranch house set in a grove of live oak trees in a valley between two mountain ranges. Two brief scenes re-create 1930s Salinas and Soledad in meticulous period detail. Though the ranch house itself is nondescript, needing a coat of paint, the scenes of ranch life evoke nostalgia for a more innocent world of idyllic beauty, perhaps too much so, for to some extent the beauty and the sense of comradeship among men working together, eating outdoors on trestle tables, and pitching horseshoes undermine all the talk of loneliness as well as the bleakness of the Depression.

The screenplay is by Horton Foote, a specialist in Americana, whose credits include screenplays for *To Kill a Mockingbird* and stories by William Faulkner and Flannery O'Connor as well as *Tender Mercies* and *A Trip to Bountiful*. Foote would seem a good choice, and for the most part he keeps Steinbeck's dialogue intact, not tampering with it but simply finding ways of opening up the settings so that the action is not mostly confined to the bunkhouse. The film begins inside a moving boxcar, in which the flickering light dimly reveals a man hunched over; at the end, we realize that what we are seeing is

George traveling alone after killing Lennie. After the opening credits, shown on the interior boxcar walls instead of on the exterior as in Milestone's film, the camera cuts to a woman in a torn red dress running and screaming in one direction and to George and Lennie running the other way. Pursued by horsemen and dogs, they hide in a stream, submerged and hidden by overhanging grasses; once the way is clear, they run and catch a passing freight train.

Thereafter, for the most part, Foote just follows Steinbeck's text for the play, but in two instances he makes curious omissions that are damaging rather than an improvement. When Lennie intrudes in the room of Crooks, the ranch's solitary black, the dialogue follows Steinbeck through Crooks's initial resentment, his taunting Lennie with the idea that George might never come back, Lennie's rage, and Crooks's placating him, but it cuts off the scene before Crooks can find out about the plan to buy a small farm that can be a refuge from loneliness and dependency and ask to join George, Lennie, and Candy there. And at the end, George shoots Lennie on the line "And I get to tend the rabbits"; the rest of the dialogue, in which George has Lennie look across the river while he describes a heaven in which there will be no trouble, fighting, or pain and then kills Lennie as he says ecstatically, "I can see it!" is cut. The shooting is photographed in a medium long shot, in which we cannot see fully either Lennie's happiness or George's agony, further muting the emotional intensity of the ending.

The film is also less moving than its predecessors because of the performances by the two leads. As George, Gary Sinise (though 37 in actuality) seems too young and handsome, a point that Curley's wife comments on, and as Peter Rainer of the *Los Angeles Times* observed, his performance is "too reined in," so that we don't sufficiently see and become involved in his pain, his attachment to Lennie, the intensity of his dream for the promised land.[45] As Lennie, John Malkovich is sympathetic but not lovable. Partly, he is physically off-putting—bald, with a mouthful of rotting teeth that rather spoil his smile, and with a high, singsong, childish voice. At moments, he is scary, like a Frankenstein monster; his smashing Curley's hand is particularly vivid, as we see Curley thrash-ing in unbelievable agony, and the killing of Curley's wife is equally terrifying, not just a big, harmless kid losing control. The interpretation is valid and consistent, but Malkovich is a highly intellectual performer, and he has not entirely managed to subdue his intellectuality in the characterization. As Vincent Canby observed, "Everything about the performance has been intelligently thought out.... The actor's intelligence, however, shows through."[46]

The other performances are fine, especially Ray Walston's as Candy. Walston made his reputation as a comic, but here he is a grizzled, believable Candy, not quite so moving as Lew Ayres but fine nevertheless, especially in the scenes with his old dog. Casey Siemaszko brings out not only Curley's nastiness but also the insecurity behind it. As his wife (not called Mae this time), Sherilyn Fenn is not the slattern that Cassie Yates made her; instead she looks like the pretty girl in 1930s Coca-Cola ads. Yates stressed her loneliness, but Fenn makes her flirtatious, moving her legs provocatively, pulling up her short skirts to show the lace hem of her slip. Both some changes in dialogue and Sinise's direction and acting make George obviously more responsive to her, not so much in what he says (though he does not call her a tart and tells her off less) but in an evident attraction that he represses with some difficulty. John Terry is a strong, stalwart Slim, and the bunkhouse boys are utterly believable. But Joe Morton's Crooks lacks the dignity that Leigh Whipper brought to the part in 1939; while tormenting Lennie, he comes across as a "baad" black that is almost a stereotype.

At the end, it is unrealistic to have all the ranch hands gallop off on horseback as a posse. Most of them probably would not have learned to ride that well, if at all; they are, after all, peons, and Curley has used his solitary horsemanship to demonstrate his mastery over them. Nor is it likely that the ranch would have a dozen or so saddle horses all ready to go. Furthermore, all the galloping to and fro distracts from the poignancy of Lennie's end. After his death, we return to the inside of the boxcar with George huddled in solitary misery, after which the film cuts to shots of George and Lennie bucking barley and then walking off together—a reprise of the 1980 ending but handled less sentimentally.

There is much to admire in the 1992 film, yet it is vaguely unsatisfying. It is not so emotionally involving as its 1939 and 1980 predecessors or apparently the stage production that reduced a teenage Gary Sinise to tears and made him determined to become an actor.

Meanwhile, the play seems to go on forever. It continues to be revived frequently and widely. Thus, writing a work simultaneously as a novel and a play produced positive dividends. One does not ordinarily think of Steinbeck as a playwright, but *Of Mice and Men* has become an enduring classic of the American stage and screen, one of the best plays written in America. That is no small accomplishment.

9

MIMI REISEL GLADSTEIN

The Grapes of Wrath
Steinbeck and the Eternal Immigrant

The many conferences and publications honoring the fiftieth anniversary of *The Grapes of Wrath* in 1989 give strong indication of the durability of John Steinbeck's world-famous novel. There are still a few holdouts such as Leslie Fiedler, who fudges his condemnation of this "problematic middlebrow book" by allowing the "ambiguous, archetypal final scene" to "redeem" the work,[1] but even hardened Steinbeck-basher Harold Bloom concedes that "no canonical standards worthy of human respect could exclude *The Grapes of Wrath* from a serious reader's esteem." And while expressing his reservations, Bloom is still "grateful for the novel's continued existence."[2]

If further assurance is needed, and I think it is not, of the book's continued and continuing significance, the success of the Steppenwolf Theatre Company production of *The Grapes of Wrath* in Chicago, La Jolla, London, and on Broadway adds evidence of the ability of the story to capture new audiences. Frank Galati's adaptation of Steinbeck's novel has elicited a chorus of praise from critics, each with his or her own explanation of the reason why Steinbeck's timely tale of a problem in the 1930s continues to engage us in the 1990s. To this end, the *USA Today* article about the production was headlined "New *Grapes* Still Bears Fruit."[3] Terry Kinney, the actor who plays Jim Casy in the Steppenwolf production, sees parallels between the problem of the homeless in New York's East Village and the story of the Joads.[4] A review by David Patrick Stearns connects Steinbeck's "surprisingly timely message" with how "we deal with holocaust."[5] Like Kinney, Mimi Kramer, in her review in the *New Yorker*, claims that *The Grapes of Wrath* is about homelessness, but what she describes is a more general homelessness, which, in her opinion, characterizes all great American epics, including *Gone with the Wind, Moby-Dick,* and on another level *The Wizard of Oz.*[6] Alan Brinkley's response to his own question of "Why Steinbeck's Okies Speak to Us Today" is that Steinbeck's message is of the importance of a "transcendent community" that Brinkley links to both modern radicalism and conservatism, citing former President George Bush's "thousand points of light" as a contemporary expression of a call to transcendent community.[7]

Kinney, Stearns, Kramer, and Brinkley all posit acceptable explanations for the lasting quality of Steinbeck's novel. Each of their theories adds its own illumination to Steinbeck's story. And this is appropriate, because Steinbeck described *The Grapes of Wrath* as a five-layered book, explaining that "a reader will find as many as he can and won't find more than he has in himself."[8]

I would like to suggest yet a different layer in Steinbeck's novel, a layer that, at Steinbeck's suggestion, I found in myself. It is a layer that, like the other layers, readers have found in themselves; it explains a significant portion of the book's continuing and universal appeal, because if *The Grapes of Wrath* is about homelessness, if it is about the exploitation of an underclass by the power structure, and if it is the American equivalent of the exodus from Egypt, as various writers have suggested, it is also the story of a quintessential American experience.

And it is more than that. For while the immigrant's experience can be categorized on a personal level and also be seen as a national paradigm, it is not just in America that *The Grapes of Wrath* endures. Steinbeck's pages communicate to a worldwide audience, as the Third International Steinbeck Congress and the Steinbeck Conference held in October 1989 in Moscow illustrate. And while there are as many reasons for the novel's worldwide appeal as there are for its American appeal, perhaps the theme of the eternal immigrant is another reason why the story of the Joads speaks to such varying audiences. For the problems faced by immigrants are international. Peoples move, boundaries change, economic and political problems create migrations. The Oklahomans in California are like the Chinese in Malaysia, the Indians in South Africa, the Turkish in Germany, or the Algerians in France. Professor Jin Young Choi, speaking on "Steinbeck Studies in Korea" on the first day of the Third International Steinbeck Congress, commented on the parallels between Steinbeck's Okies and Korean farmers who moved to Manchuria. Her evocation of the empathy with which the Korean psyche, educated by the experiences of Korean immigrants in China, Japan, and Manchuria, is keyed to the suffering of the displaced provides yet another piece of evidence in the case I wish to build. My thesis, then, is that the Joads gain much of their literary cachet from the similarities of the problems suffered by immigrants everywhere. Their experience is universal.

At first, when Steinbeck was writing his "Harvest Gypsies" series of articles for the *San Francisco News*, neither he nor the editorial staff of that newspaper saw the Dust Bowl migrants as analogous to the previous groups of immigrants who had been exploited by California's agricultural industry. Because they were American citizens, Steinbeck expected that the newcomers would be treated differently from the immigrant or foreign labor that California had imported in the past. In his newspaper series, Steinbeck describes them as "the best American stock, intelligent, resourceful, and if given a chance, socially responsible."[9] The editorial that accompanied his articles stated, "They cannot be handled as the Japanese, Mexicans, and Filipinos."[10] These prophesies proved false.

Putting aside the question of whether or not these opinions are, in themselves, nationalistic or racist, for purposes of this discussion, the significant fact is that by the time Steinbeck finished *The Grapes of Wrath*, less than three years later, he had learned that xenophobia does not discriminate between migrants and immigrants, between light skin and dark. What he saw in the years between the publication of the articles and the completion of the novel found its way into his fictional narrative and clearly illustrated that, in terms of what they encountered in California, this "best American stock" was treated the same as any immigrant stock.

Steinbeck's awareness of this is communicated both subtly and pointedly. In chapter 19, one of the interchapters where he expresses the mood of the Californians during this period and their hostile attitude toward drought refugees, his narration leaves little doubt that the Oklahomans are perceived as aliens, not countrymen. Steinbeck depicts a scene where a deputy sheriff tramples the small, secret garden of one of the migrant workers. We enter the sheriff's thoughts as he kicks off the heads of turnip greens. "Outlanders," he thinks, "foreigners."[11] His reason recoils from this untruth, but it is no match for his emotions, which rationalize his actions by explaining, "Sure, they talk the same language, but they ain't the same" (*GOW*, p. 322).

The sheriff is one individual, but in the narrative Steinbeck also imagines the thought patterns of the general community. In these passages is more evidence that the newcomers are considered foreigners. To excuse their brutality toward the migrants, the citizens who run the communities project a possible uprising among the Okies. In their collective paranoia, they fear that the farm laborers might retaliate against their harsh treatment, might march against their oppressors as "the Lombards did in Italy, as the Germans did in Gaul, and the Turks in Byzantium" (*GOW*, p. 323). Clearly, the images in the Californians' minds equate the Okies with foreigners.

Chapter 19 is one of the most clearly articulated instances in which Steinbeck's narrative demonstrates that he understood that the Oklahomans were more immigrant than migrant in the minds of his fellow Californians. But he also develops the idea dramatically through his narrative. In the Joad family scenes, he shows us the Joads experiencing what immigrants have borne throughout history.

To fully develop parallels between the Joad family experiences and the experiences of immigrant groups throughout the world, I would need a book-length manuscript. For the purposes of this essay, I have chosen to illustrate parallels to one or two immigrant groups, hoping that in the variety of my examples, the particular will establish the universal.[12]

At the heart of every immigrant's experience is a dream—a vision of hope that is embodied in his or her destination. Americans have long seen their country as the land of opportunity, and the vision carried in the hearts of most immigrants who have come here is of the *goldeneh medina*, a place where the streets are paved with gold. For every immigrant is impelled by the expectation of a better life at his or her journey's end. What else but such a vision could entice Haitians to brave stormy seas on rickety rafts, the Vietnamese boat people, the Marielitos, Mexican boys to allow themselves to be locked into suffocating boxcars? Similarly, the Joads embark upon a hazardous journey, their overburdened truck like a rickety raft, the Arizona and California deserts seas of sand rather than water. The gold at the end of their journey is embodied in the orange groves of California rather than the imagined gold-paved streets of New York. Ma's vision is of a place "never cold. An' fruit ever' place, an' people just bein' in the nicest places, little white houses in among the orange trees. . . . An' the little fellas go out an' pick oranges right off the tree" (*GOW*, p. 124). Ma's dream vision, where gold/oranges hang on the trees (lie in the streets) just for the taking, is an archetypal immigrant fantasy.

For Ma the oranges represent more than gold; they represent the luxury and nourishment of the Promised Land. In her vision, oranges are abundant "ever' place" and readily accessible, "right off the tree." Orange trees do not grow in Oklahoma, so oranges are also a bit of a delicacy. For my father, who was raised in Poland, the symbol was bananas, a great luxury in that cold country. When he was told that bananas were sold at five cents a stalk in Nicaragua, the country he first immigrated to, he thought it must be a land of unimagined luxury and abundance.

For Grampa Joad, in the novel, the synecdoche is more biblical. California is where he can "get a whole bunch of grapes" and "squash 'em on my face an' let 'em run offen my chin" (*GOW*, p. 112). Fruit, be it oranges, grapes, or bananas, is a universal symbol for abundance and luxury. Maybe that is why the horn of plenty is filled with it.

The immigrant's dream is often unrealistic, and extravagant

expectations can lead to bitter disappointment. Steinbeck fore-shadows this in his novel. Even Ma, who acts as the cheer-leader for the venture, has her moments of doubt. She says to Tom, "I'm scared of stuff so nice. I ain't got faith. I'm scared somepin ain' so nice about it" (*GOW*, p. 123). Faced with the reality of pulling up roots and leaving his and his ancestors' home ground, Grampa rejects his promised luxury: "I don't give a goddamn if they's oranges an' grapes crowdin' a fella outa bed even" (p. 152). The dream turns to ashes as the nourishing oranges and grapes become "winfall" peaches that, rather than providing sustenance, cause "the skitters." My father's bitter lesson came when, having bought several stalks of five-cent bananas at the dock the minute his boat landed, he discovered that a stalk of bananas cost only two cents in the city.

It is characteristic of the immigrant experience that immi-grants garner no credit for either family or nationality contri-butions to the history and culture of the country into which they travel. This is a truth Italian-Americans know well. It mattered not that the Americas were both discovered by and named for Italians: Columbus's and Vespucci's countrymen were not greeted warmly nor treated well as immigrants. As one Italian immigrant noted, they were only expected to per-form "all the manual and menial work the older Americans spurned."[13] Steinbeck also notes that past contributions have no bearing on present treatment when he has the general voice of the migrants explain, "One of our folks was in the Revolu-tion, an' they was lots of our folks in the Civil War—both sides" (*GOW*, p. 318). Ma also boasts about the Joad lineage: "We're Joads. We don't look up to nobody. Grampa's grampa, he fit in the Revolution" (p. 420). These credentials are ignored by the Californians.

Another aspect of the immigrant experience that echoes from the pages of *The Grapes of Wrath* is the propensity for finding a derogatory term with which to label the new arrival. Contemporary sociology books define this as an "ethnophaulism."[14] The term carries with it deprecatory stereotypes and negative images. And the world learned the term "Okies" from Steinbeck. The term became so well known that my immigrant father was bemused when I brought home what he referred to jokingly as an "Okie" to marry. He expected a rube, driving a laden-down jalopy. The image of the "Okie" as beaten-down loser was so pervasive that the Board of Regents of the University of Oklahoma came up with the idea of creating a championship football team as an antidote for the statewide depression caused by Steinbeck's book.[15]

In the novel, Tom first hears the word from a man who, returning from California, tells him, "You never been called 'Okie' yet." Tom doesn't know what the word means. He asks, "Okie? What's that?" The man responds, "Well, Okie use' ta mean you was from Oklahoma. Now it means you're a dirty son-of-a-bitch. Okie means you're scum" (*GOW*, p. 280). Tom's reaction to the term is like that of the young protagonist in an autobiographical short story by Chicano writer John Rechy. In "El Paso del Norte" Rechy speaks of the hatred in Texas for Mexicans. In grammar school his protagonist is called "Mexicangreaser, Mexicangreaser." The boy is perplexed and says, "Well, yes my mother did do an awful lot of frying but we never put any grease on our hair and so it bothered me."[16] Each immigrant group has experienced its share of such epithets, complete with the stereotypes that accompany them. The effect is soul-withering. Even the redoubtable Ma is unnerved by the epithet. Her interchange with the policeman who first uses the term on her illustrates both the negative effect of the name-calling and the fact that Ma sees herself as coming from a different country than his.

The policeman begins by saying to Ma, "We don't want none of you settlin' down here." Ma's response is anger. She picks up an iron skillet and advances on the man. When he loosens his gun, she rejoins, "Go ahead. . . . Scarin' women. I'm thankful the men folks ain't here. They'd tear you to pieces. *In my country* [emphasis mine] you watch your tongue." It is at this point that the man responds, "Well, *you ain't in your country* [emphasis mine] now. You're in California, an' we don't want you goddamn Okies settlin' down" (*GOW*, p. 291). Note that both Ma and the policeman see themselves as coming from different countries, not as citizens of the same country. At this point in the interchange Ma's advance is stopped. It is not the gun that stops her, but the effect of the name-calling: "She looked puzzled. 'Okies?' she said softly. 'Okies'" (p. 291). When the man leaves, Ma has to fight with her face to keep from breaking down. The effect is so devastating that Rose of Sharon pretends to be asleep (p. 292).

Hungarians have been called "hunkies," Bohemians "bo-hunks," Chinese "chinks," and Italians "dagos." Ethnophaulisms exist for every kind of immigrant, regardless of race or country of origin. In scenes such as the one between Ma and the policeman, Steinbeck shows that he understands the effects of this kind of name-calling. He shows his Californians behaving toward the new arrivals in ways that are typical of the in-group's behavior toward the out-group. He is particularly adept at underlining the distance between the behavior of the out-group and the way that behavior is perceived by the in-group. This he does with caustic dramatic irony. In one instance, the reader has just finished a scene in which the Joads act unusually compassionately and charitably. They, who have so few resources, give part of what they have to people who are neither kin nor longtime friends. Pa takes "two crushed bills" from his purse and leaves them, together with a half sack of potatoes and a quarter of a keg of salt pork that Ma has put by, for the Wilsons (*GOW*, p. 299). After this remarkable act of charity, their next stop is a service station in Needles. The service station attendant does not see the Joads that Steinbeck has just shown the reader. He sees only their determination, which he translates into hardness, describing them to his helper as "a hard-looking outfit." His helper provides the stereotype: "Them Okies? They're all hard-lookin'" (p. 301). Then he goes on to make statements that reveal the depth of his prejudice, a prejudice expressed toward this group of Anglo-American migrants, but one remarkably similar to the prejudices expressed toward many immigrant groups.

One of the cruel ironies of the treatment of immigrant groups is that they are paid lower wages, given poorer working conditions, limited to uninhabitable living quarters, and then despised as being subhuman because they live as they do. Steinbeck has his service station boy say, "Them goddamn Okies got no sense and no feeling. They ain't human. A human being wouldn't live like they do. A human being couldn't stand it to be so dirty and miserable. They ain't a hell of a lot better than gorillas" (*GOW*, p. 301). The universality of this kind of negative stereotyping is almost too obvious for commentary. It is the kind of thinking that allows the killing of "gooks" because they aren't seen as human, the lynching of "niggers" because they are seen as an inferior species.

Steinbeck shows numerous instances of the Okies being treated as less than human. Although Floyd, a man the Joads meet in the first Hooverville camp, does little more than ask the contractor about his license and pay scale, the deputy shoots at Floyd when he runs from possible incarceration. Only the most blatant disregard for the bystanders could produce such a response by the deputies, as lawmen are taught to hold their fire in a crowd. Steinbeck's narrative makes it clear that Floyd is dodging in and out of sight in a crowd of people when the deputy fires (*GOW*, p. 361). The result is horrible. A woman's hand is shattered. This has no effect on the deputy, who "raised his gun again" (p. 361). At this point, Casy kicks him in the neck. The woman is hysterical, with blood oozing from her wound. When the rest of the deputy's group arrives and Casy tells them that the deputy hit a woman, they show no interest in her. Even when Casy says, "They's a woman down the row like to bleed to death from his bad shootin'," their response is: "We'll see about that later" (p. 364). After Casy reminds them a third time, they finally go to take a look. Their behavior, which up to this point is totally devoid of responsibility, is compounded by insensitivity and lack of humanity. They do not see a woman, another human being. They only see the "mess a .45 does make" (p. 364).

Because of their powerlessness and because they are seen as less than human, immigrants are often housed apart and in dehumanizing facilities. This has been true since medieval times, when immigrants were relegated to the outskirts of the city, the most dangerous area in those days because it was most vulnerable to attack. In an ironic reversal, today's most dangerous areas are the inner cities, where ghettos are most often located. This "segregation" or "ghettoization" is called "spatial segregation" in contemporary sociological studies. Steinbeck's Okies are subjected to this "spatial segregation." They are not allowed to settle where they like but are shunted to the Hoovervilles, impermanent shantytowns of tents and shacks. And even these miserable communities are seen as threatening by the xenophobic citizens. The first Hooverville the Joads stay in is burned so its inhabitants must move on. The burning of ghettos, or shtetls, was common, and was sometimes responsible for creating immigrants, as in the fictional Anatevka of *Fiddler on the Roof*, which had many real-life analogues.

When the migrant workers are given housing by the companies that hire them, the living conditions are appalling. Universally, living conditions and working conditions that immigrant and migrant workers must endure are disgraceful. The burning to death of the young garment workers who were locked up in the loft is a historical instance of the abusive working conditions immigrants suffered. When the Joads go to pick peaches, they are, for all intents and purposes, locked in. A police escort ushers them in, a guard with a shotgun sits at the end of each street (*GOW*, p. 515), and when Tom tries to go outside the camp for a walk, a guard with a gun tells him he cannot leave the compound (p. 519). The image is of a work camp—as in the Netherlands, where the Moluccans were housed in the concentration camps abandoned by the Nazis.

The house the Joads are assigned is one room for eight people, a room that smells of sweat and grease. Nor have the facilities for laboring immigrants changed much. If anything, they are worse. In a 1981 study, migrant housing is called "grotesque" and "nightmarish." The reporter says it is difficult to write about "without seeming to be melodramatic."[17] Brent Ashabrenner, in a 1985 book about Haitians, Jamaicans, and Guatemalans who, with their families, are the contemporary Okies of Florida and the South, reports similar conditions.[18]

Steinbeck leaves his immigrant family devastated by death, desertion, and flood. The last scene—Rose of Sharon's selfless act of giving—used to fill me with impatience. How ridiculous to expect that this woman, whose lack of proper nutrition and care has produced a dead baby, should have enough nourishment to sustain a dying man. What a paltry symbolic act. And yet, history has proved Steinbeck's impulse unerring. For, as Ma prophesied, the people do go on. The Okies have survived. James Gregory, in his recently published *American Exodus*, charts the durability of the Okie subculture in California today.[19]

Faced with seemingly insurmountable obstacles, immigrants the world over not only survive, but prevail. Michael Dukakis, the son of Greek immigrants, ran for president of the United States. Alberto Fujimori, son of Japanese immigrants to Peru, won the Peruvian presidency. Roberto Villareal, who as a boy picked cotton with his Mexican immigrant family in the fields of Texas, is now chairman of the Department of Political Science at the University of Texas at El Paso, my university. *The Grapes of Wrath* speaks to me, because *The Grapes of Wrath* speaks of me, an immigrant, who with my family experienced the pains and promise of immigration, an experience Steinbeck wrote of so tellingly in his story of the Joads.

10

SUSAN SHILLINGLAW

California Answers
The Grapes of Wrath

Four months after publication of *The Grapes of Wrath*, John Steinbeck responded sharply to mounting criticism of his book: "I know what I was talking about," he told a *Los Angeles Times* reporter. "I lived, off and on, with those Okies for the last three years. Anyone who tries to refute me will just become ridiculous."[1] His angry retort is largely on target—but the opposition was in earnest and had been even before his novel was published.

In 1938 corporate farmers in California responded forcefully to the consequences of continued migration: the twin threats of unions and a liberal migrant vote.[2] Beginning early that year a statewide publicity campaign to discredit the "migrant menace" had been mounted by the Associated Farmers and the newly formed CCA, or California Citizens Association, a group with the broad support of banks, oil companies, agricultural land companies, businesses, and public utilities.[3] Well-funded and well-placed, the CCA and the Associated Farmers produced scores of articles meant to discourage further migration, to encourage Dust Bowlers already in California to return to their home states, and to convince the federal government that California's migrant problem was a federal, not a state, responsibility. These articles vigorously defended farmers' wage scales and housing standards. They complained about the state's generous relief, which, at almost twice that of Oklahoma and Arkansas, had "encouraged" migration. And they often maligned the state's newest residents. "The whole design of modern life," noted an article in the *San Francisco Examiner* entitled "The Truth About California," "has stimulated their hunger for change and adventure, fun and frippery. Give them a relief check and they'll head straight for a beauty shop and a movie."[4] The publication of Steinbeck's novel in March 1939—followed shortly thereafter by Carey McWilliams's carefully documented *Factories in the Fields*— simply gave the outraged elite a new focus for their attack.

The campaign took on a new intensity. Editorials and pamphlets, many underwritten by the Associated Farmers, claimed to expose Steinbeck's "prejudice, exaggeration, and oversimplification," the thesis of one tract, or to discredit the "Termites Steinbeck and McWilliams," the title of another.[5] Of greater impact, however, were the more sustained efforts to counter what were perceived as Steinbeck's factual inaccuracies. I shall examine four of the most important respondents. Two who defended California agriculture were highly respected professional writers: Ruth Comfort Mitchell, the author of *Of Human Kindness*, and Frank J. Taylor, a free-lance journalist who covered California business, farming, and recreation for the state and national press. And two were highly successful retired farmers, to use the word loosely: Marshall V. Hartranft, the Los Angeles fruit grower and real estate developer who wrote *Grapes of Gladness: California's Refreshing and Inspiring Answer to John Steinbeck's "Grapes of Wrath,"* and Sue Sanders, touted as the "friend of the migrant," who wrote and published a tract called "The Real Causes of Our Migrant Problem." Since each contributed to what can only be called a hysterical campaign against the migrant presence and Steinbeck himself, it is difficult not to cast them as villains. What must be recognized, however, is that each with great sincerity and, to a large extent, accuracy, described another California—a brawny, confident state that bustled with entrepreneurial zeal. Each defended California against Steinbeck's charges largely by ignoring much of the agony and cruelty he chronicled. Each sought an answer to the "migrant question" without fully comprehending—or perhaps, more significantly, empathizing with—the "problem," the migrants' plight. To understand each writer's perspective is to appreciate better the intensity of the political clashes of the 1930s, a period when, as liberal activist Richard Criley observed, "Social issues were so sharp and so clear . . . we were pulled to take a position because things were so acute, so terrifying in the need to change."[6] These interpreters of the California scene resisted change.

In the late 1930s, Los Gatos novelists Ruth Comfort Mitchell (1882–1954) and John Steinbeck shared a magnificent view of the Santa Clara Valley from their mountain homes six miles apart.[7] Similarities in perspective end there. The author of sixteen novels and several collections of poems, as well as short stories and articles published in *Woman's Home Companion, Century, Good Housekeeping,* and *McCall's,* Mitchell claimed as her fictional terrain the uncertain ground of young love. When she wrote a vaudeville sketch on the "great question of labor" in 1907, it was lauded as an "uplifting" piece that helped give the stage a more wholesome image. Mitchell's play, noted the reviewer, "holds the human emotions paramount and introduces the labor and capital strike feature as secondary."[8]

That comment holds true for much of her work. Mitchell always "liked to take the bright view," noted her obituary in the *New York Times*. Neither by temperament nor by class was she fitted to fully comprehend Steinbeck's Joads. She was one of California's elite, raised in comfort and married to wealth. "I know nothing about that stimulating lash of adversity that all of you people who have had to fight for your foothold talk about," she admitted to one reporter.[9] Her only contact with migrant labor was on her husband Sanborn Young's dairy farm south of Fresno, where the two lived for several years until Young became a state senator—and notorious strike buster— in 1925.[10] As early as 1918, when they built their Los Gatos summer home, she took to wearing only green, writing on only green stationery using green ink and stamps, and driving only green cars (a pose that Steinbeck almost certainly satirizes in the effete Joe Elegant of *Sweet Thursday*, whose manuscript is on "green paper typed with a green ribbon"). Mitchell's eccentricity was seen as part of her charm, and this prolific and witty author was much in demand as a public speaker for women's groups both locally and nationally. Often she discussed writing, read her poetry, or commented on her recent work. But just as often in the late 1930s Mitchell—state president of the National Association of Pro America, a Republican women's association—lectured on international politics.

The publication of *The Grapes of Wrath* gave her a fresh platform much closer to home. As novelist, popular lecturer, wife of Farmer/Senator Young, and efficient political organizer, she was the ideal candidate to help launch a campaign against Steinbeck's novel. In league with the Associated Farmers—in fact, she gave the keynote speech at their annual convention in December 1939—she threw her considerable resources into the superbly organized attack against the novel. On August 23, 1939, the day after *Grapes* was banned in Kern County, William B. Camp, president of the Associated Farmers, announced a statewide plan to recall the book.[11] In that same week, Mitchell was chair and key speaker at a meeting of Pro America in San Francisco, where "five hundred persons . . . heard speakers denounce recent books dealing with California's migrant problem, call for cessation of relief for transients, and praise efforts of individual farmers to better conditions for migratory workers."[12] This meeting may serve as a touchstone for all such gatherings and may demonstrate why Steinbeck could with truth call the "Ass Farmers"—his term—ridiculous. It was here that Mitchell contended that California farms were becoming smaller, and another speaker maintained that "farmworkers of California are better paid and better housed than agricultural workers anywhere else in the world."[13]

Even if such exaggerated claims characterized many attacks on the novel, it cannot be said that defenses of California agriculture rested on overstatement alone. The central thrust was not to ban Steinbeck's text statewide, although some in Kern County attempted to do so, or to discredit the man, although many tried. Rather, it was to replace one picture of California farm and migrant life with another. Mitchell set out to prove that California was a rural paradise, farmed by energetic, committed Americans. In June 1939 she began writing what became the longest and most highly publicized response to *Grapes*, her novel *Of Human Kindness*, published by D. Appleton-Century Company in 1940. As she was writing her book, she repeatedly declared to audiences and reporters that she told "the other side of the story," insisting that in doing so she did not intend to attack Steinbeck, merely to defend the ranchers' position. Indeed, both she and her publisher took pains to dissociate her book from Steinbeck's. Her novel, she asserted, was fully outlined before Steinbeck's book was published. But this seems unlikely, since Mitchell's novel is crafted to dovetail with the Associated Farmers' own campaign.[14]

In their many tracts the farmer is invariably a heroic figure, a hard-working man protecting his home and minimal profits, enduring the uncertainties of weather and insects that affected his crops. Prolific pamphleteer Philip Bancroft, farmer and Republican candidate for the state senate in 1938, described himself as enjoying the "out-of-doors life, simply and economically."[15] Cut from the same cloth, Ed Banner, Mitchell's dairyman farmer, is as patriotic as his last name suggests—a point hammered home by his daughter's fiancé, who calls her "Star Spangled." The Banners are "San Joaquin Valley pioneers, third generation in California; plain people, poor people, proud people; salt of the earth."[16] Their success, as Mitchell never tires of making clear, was achieved not through wealth, but by working "sixteen hours out of the twenty four." Indeed, the Banner matriarch "out-earth mothers" Ma Joad, thus proving the family's superior Americanism; she is supremely fair-minded, a "Dowager Empress in her authority, her calm, her composure, her wisdom. Old Buddha in a faded gingham dress" (*OHK*, p. 72). And she is altruistic to a fault: her own home is "less good than the cabins she had built for her men." Their farm community is similarly archetypal: poor but energetic, closely knit and supportive—the neighbors banding together to help the Banners clean their new house and to break up, rather gently, a strike.

In presenting the "other side," Mitchell takes pains to show that farm life, like migrant life, could be "hard and harsh and uncompromising" (*OHK*, p. 75). Only one farmer enjoys wealth and leisure, and he is compared to Simon Legree. This benighted farmer is "always undercutting the prevailing wage, charging them fifteen cents to ride out to the field, [and building] shacks a self-respecting pig wouldn't live in" (p. 221). But this "blood-sucker," "gorilla," and wife tormenter, Mitchell shows, is far from the norm.

This rural tycoon is as exaggerated a type as are the interlopers who threaten Arcadia. One Okie, Lute Willow, the "okie-dokie Boy," intrudes and elopes with the Banner daughter. But the guitar-slinging Lute is hardly representative. His family owns a dairy farm in Oklahoma, and he came to California by choice, not because he was driven out of his home. Most significantly, under Ed Banner's tutelage he learns to work hard. And so Ed, initially rejecting the "dumb and shiftless" Okies, learns to accept this superior specimen. Mitchell's point is clear: a few migrants can be integrated into the valley communities if they are willing to work as diligently as have the farmers—precisely the Associated Farmers' announced position. In "The Truth about John Steinbeck and the Migrants," the laborers are said not to be the "beasts" Steinbeck portrays, but "honest, intelligent, and assimilable people."[17]

Neither Mitchell nor her supporters, however, were prepared to accept leftists who, they charged, entered the state only to inflame the workers. Most "replies" condemned the Communists. In Mitchell's text, the chief spokeswoman for what is clearly perceived as Steinbeck's position is a new history teacher who looks like a rabbit. Rude, flat-chested, sallow, and lesbian, Pinky Emory corrupts the valley children—the Banner son included—by arguing that migrants were "lured out to California by the farmers so oodles and oodles would come and they could get cheap labor and pay starvation wages!" (*OHK*, p. 81). This is, of course, Steinbeck's novel in a nutshell. There is also a union organizer, a "Carmen—and Delilah—Borgia" (p. 206), a "Black Widow" (perhaps modeled on labor organizer Caroline Decker),[18] who seduces the son, betrays the history teacher who adores her, and, after sending Pinky to her death, seizes her body and uses it to inspire the workers to action in a scene that echoes Mac's reaction to Joy's death in *In Dubious Battle*. The organizers are clearly a bad lot whose sexual deviance redundantly condemns their already perverse politics. As Philip Bancroft had earlier noted in an article characterizing the Communists: "Some of the most rabid and dangerous are attractive and educated women."[19] For Mitchell, the women's position is synonymous with Steinbeck's, and their siren songs are as fatal as his text. Indeed, what may have been most inflammatory about *Grapes* was its sympathy with collective action. In championing the "family of man" Steinbeck seemed perilously close to embracing a socialist ideal, and Mitchell, like all these interpreters, would not betray her faith in American individualism, its excesses notwithstanding.

What may be most remarkable about Mitchell's novel, however, is not her sublimely ridiculous characters—the noble farmers, sapphic leftist organizers, and uniquely respectable Okie—all of whom she judges against the Banner ethos and the rhetoric of the Associated Farmers. Rather, it is that, while waving the virtuous Banners—Ed and Mary—so vigorously before the reader, Mitchell nonetheless proclaims her objectivity. Clearly she wants the reader to believe that her novel is grounded, not in the self-interest of the landed class, but in fair-mindedness. Not merely a narrative stance, fair-mindedness is realized by her strong female characters: the Banner matriarch, Helga the public nurse, and the semiautobiographical heroine, Mary Banner, whose perspective is the broadest in the book. Armed with an urban education and a rural practicality, Mary—like Mitchell herself— "bend[s] over backwards trying to be fair" (*OHK*, p. 221). (It was an acrobatic attitude many pamphleteers also assumed.) Thus, Mary articulates the book's (and, to a large extent, the Associated Farmers') central tenet: "I know just as well as you do that there's injustice and graft and greed here and everywhere, and ignorance and filth and suffering, but it's utterly false to say the world isn't better and going to be still better!" (pp. 178–79). And it is the farmers, not the staid city dwellers, who are most open to the meliorism she envisions, even though such change is gradual and often slow. When the students picket in support of their teacher, the politically chromatic Pinky, it is a farmer who tells the others that "most of us are too far to the right. We've got to do some fact-facing ourselves" (p. 190). Later, the feisty Ed Banner, initially denouncing the Okies, learns to accept both his Okie son-in-law and his own political obligation to run for the state senate. For Mitchell, it is axiomatic that good farmers adapt. Hard and demanding rural life molds fair-mindedness. This seems to be Mitchell's central position, the objective "other side" she championed against the "prejudice, exaggeration, and oversimplification" seen in *Grapes*.

If Mitchell best articulated the Associated Farmers' position in fiction, Frank J. Taylor, free-lance journalist, was the farmers' most formidable advocate in nonfiction. Taylor (1894– 1972) also attended the Pro America evening at the Palace Hotel in San Francisco late in the summer of 1939. For the previous ten years, he had covered the West Coast for national magazines, first writing articles on Yellowstone and the National Park Service, and then, as a self-styled "roving reporter" for the conservative *Country Gentleman*, covering California agriculture. Being a "scout for farming stories," he notes in an autobiographical piece, "quite naturally turned up some characters who were good material for the *Sat Eve Post, Colliers, Nation's Business*, and the *Reader's Digest*. These stories had to be slanted at people who lived in cities, rather than at farmers, who were the Gent's readers."[20] Writing for these conservative national magazines and an urban audience, Taylor excelled in human interest stories about California entrepreneurs: beekeepers, vintners, and firework makers; the Burpees of seed company fame; UC Berkeley's Dr. Gericke, originator of "soil-less crops"; Walt Disney; and "Mr. Gump— of Gump's."[21] Taylor was a dyed-in-the-wool California booster. He admired the "shrewd individualists" who shaped the "Many Californias," men who wrested sizable fortunes from flowers, gold mines, and Oriental art, men who forged the state's cooperative farming and shipping interests. His perspective was, in fact, nearly identical to Mitchell's: positive, forward-looking, and pragmatic. Living and working in "the biggest and best" state, he looked around for what made it run smoothly.

Farmers did. As his 1938 article "The Merritt System" makes clear, Taylor champions the farmer's work ethic as vigorously as does Mitchell. The Merritts, father and son, owned the huge Tagus Ranch, probable site of Steinbeck's *In Dubious Battle*. But Taylor's ranch is most definitely not Steinbeck's. The benevolent Merritts "brought to farming the restless search for efficiency the elder Merritt had learned in the industrial world, and they have made Tagus Ranch a year-round producer." Furthermore, Taylor notes that they have created a utopian community for their workers, who live in "glistening white" houses they rent for two to four dollars a month, buy food from a company store at "chain store prices" (where the "Merritts manage to lose a cent or two on every dollar of sales—purposely"), and send their children to the Tagus school, where they are given cod-liver oil if they appear malnourished despite the hot chocolate and graham crackers they are fed at recess.

The only flies in the ointment, reports Taylor, are the "radical labor organizers" who, seemingly without cause, "descended in force on Tagus Ranch" a few years earlier and "dragged fruit pickers from their ladders [and] threatened women and children." And, in a note at the end, he reports that the Merritts also have problems with Okies who are so accustomed to living in one-room shacks that they "chopped out partitions" in the cottages and "burned them when firewood was free for the cutting."[22] Clearly, Taylor admires the Merritts' industry and perceived goodwill toward workers. His detailed account of housing conditions is meant to counter frequent charges that farmers provided only substandard housing for workers. If Steinbeck looked for and found squalor, Taylor, like Mitchell, looked for and found the benevolent master.

He featured other farmer-entrepreneurs. In 1935, he published an equally glowing piece on "Teague of California," a wealthy man and "a farmer from the soil up . . . [who] wrested a sizable fortune from the California soil, starting with nothing in the way of assets but energy and ability and a willingness to work."[23] For Taylor, the Merritts and Teague were not capitalists but Jeffersonian gentlemen farmers, benevolent men, Horatio Algers of the soil. Yearly, they courageously faced uncertainties of weather or labor unrest; they were "beset even in times of industrial tranquility by unusual hazards such as long-haul freight rates, danger of spoiling, cost of packing, and whimsies of the market."[24] But farmers endured, a point Taylor reiterates in several articles. As American icons, these energetic, courageous, and generous owners ("Mr. Teague has never received a red cent for the vast amount of time he has devoted to the citrus and walnut cooperatives") shaped California's destiny, and their produce helped make California farming vital to the nation's economy. To threaten their crops was to steal food from tables across America.

Communist organizers are thus, for Taylor as for Mitchell, serpents in the garden. Prior to 1939 Taylor wrote several articles on the labor situation in California. No reactionary, he does not denounce unions; indeed, he features businessmen who have learned to "play ball" with unions. Nor is he unsympathetic to workers, to the Okies' "natural urge" to "dig their toes into a patch of ground . . . and settle down."[25] What he, like so many Californians, could not tolerate was the organized threat to commerce—particularly agriculture. "Communists," he declared in a 1937 article on the Associated Farmers, "had singled out California agriculture for special attention because of the vulnerable nature of its perishable crops."[26] Thus, for Taylor, the farmers, who quite naturally rose to defend the land and their rights to market their produce, were the "minute men of California agriculture." In the Salinas lettuce strike of 1936, they "transformed themselves into bands of embattled farmers, armed and imbued with a Bunker Hill determination to fight it out."[27] Taylor's metaphors define his sympathies. For him, as for Mitchell, the Associated Farmers defended the homeland against aliens— and often the issue of unfair wages was simply ignored or dismissed.

After publication of *Grapes*, DeWitt Wallace, the editor of *Reader's Digest*, asked Taylor to "trace the travels of the Joad family" in order to "tell the rest of the world about California."[28] The resulting piece, published in both *Forum* and *Reader's Digest* in November 1939, is an impressively detailed defense, supported by statistics and by Taylor's own observations. He begins, "I made one inquiry during the winter of 1937–38, following the flood which Steinbeck describes; I made another at the height of the harvest this year."[29] What he sees on both trips—and in his fifteen-year residence in the Santa Clara Valley—are the migrants as field workers, "stoops," the lower class. During both trips, he is most impressed, not by the migrants' plight but by the state's relief efforts. And he is most interested in the health officials' responses to the migrants; at least one of them, Dr. Lee Stone of Madera County, was a virulent Okie hater. His reputation for scrupulous reporting notwithstanding, Taylor could not fully acknowledge the human misery that Steinbeck had seen in his two years of trips, nor could he bear witness to the tragic flooding in the spring of 1938. Undoubtedly well intentioned, Taylor, quite simply, shared Mitchell's elitest perspective. For these two, as for the majority of Californians, field workers were—and in fact still are—an invisible population. When the state was finally forced in 1938 to acknowledge the numbers of the Dust Bowl migrants and, unlike the Mexican workers they replaced, their determination to settle in California, most Californians could hardly be expected to see the state's newest residents objectively.

To bolster his own observations, Taylor marshalled impressive statistics to show that the migrants' lot was not "the bitter fate described in *The Grapes of Wrath*." California wages, he notes, were higher than those in the southwestern states. Often true, but the cost of living was also higher. Relief payments in California, he continues, were almost twice as high as those in southwestern states, and thus migrants swarmed to California to claim this "comparative bonanza" ("CGOW," p. 233), which they were allowed after a year's residency. True, payments were higher, but, as Walter Stein observes, what many "neglected to admit was the critical role the Okie influx played in keeping wages so low that local residents actually lost money if they went off relief in order to pick the crops."[30] In addition, recent studies have shown that relief payments were not the key consideration in the migrant movement westward.[31]

To further demonstrate that migrants were well cared for, Taylor notes that during the first year, when ineligible for state relief funds, migrants could obtain emergency food and funds from the Farm Security Administration, "which maintains warehouses in eleven strategically located towns" ("CGOW," p. 233). That program, he fails to explain, had been approved only in 1938 and, more importantly, destitute migrants often could not travel, could not overcome their pride to ask for relief, could not help but fear unknown authorities. Finally, as he discusses at some length, hospitals and health facilities cared for the migrants. Like the above statistics, this was true, particularly in Kern and Madera counties. But concerned health officials could not eliminate all squalor and sickness, however impressive their efforts. Tom Collins's reports, Carey McWilliams's prose, and Dorothea Lange's portraits bear witness to the fact that outlying squatters' camps were as filthy as those in Steinbeck's novel. Both Taylor's observations and his facts demonstrate that the migrants were, for him, a group to be studied, classified. Striving for objectivity, he nonetheless accepted the Associated Farmers' absurd claims that "neither the Association nor the Bank [of America] concerns itself with wages. Rates of pay are worked out through the farmer co-operatives in each crop or through local groups" (p. 238). He recorded, as a subsequent letter to *Forum*'s editor states, "only what is profitable to his state."[32] While the solidly middle-class Steinbeck, Collins, Lange, and McWilliams saw the poor as individuals, Taylor, like so many others, viewed them primarily as a social problem.

The central point of Mitchell's argument is the farmers' integrity, while Taylor's "defense" rests chiefly on the state and federal governments' benevolence to the migrants. Yet another emphasis is to be found in *Grapes of Gladness*, a book by the retired realtor and grower Marshall V. Hartranft, whose text underscores the migrants' potential for a self-sufficient existence. "Two men looked out from their prison bars," states the epigraph to the text. "One saw the mud, the other the stars."[33] Hartranft opts for stargazing and, cursing the mudgazer "Steinbitch," invokes the spirit of Thoreau to prove that migrants can claim their own bit of land and become self-supporting.

Only Hartranft's enthusiasm for bountiful California qualified him as respondent to *Grapes*. As a fruit grower near Los Angeles he had been, in 1893, the first to sell at auction West Coast oranges to the East Coast market; subsequently, he settled in Los Angeles and founded horticultural trade dailies, the Los Angeles and the New York *Daily Fruit World*, which helped in "advertising the distinctive products of California and advancing the interests of the producers."[34] More significantly, as a Los Angeles real estate agent, he was "instrumental in the development of many of the state's large farming lands," primarily through the California Home Extension Association, which encouraged "group colonization" of desert lands. In his book, he sets out to prove Steinbeck wrong by enthusiastically summarizing his life's two projects—colonizing and cultivating California.

If the migrants' plight were taken out of the politicians'

hands, he declares in the Foreword, and put into the hands of social engineers like himself, the Joads would settle as happily in California as do his own "authentic" family, the Hoags of Beaver, Oklahoma. Traveling west, the Hoags by some good fortune continue toward Los Angeles rather than swinging to the north. Highway 66 is their road to glory, papered with signs announcing the availability of "garden acres." "Population creates land values," these posters declare, as did Hartranft whenever founding one of his several land colonies. "We will loan an acre farm to any enterprising family of worthy American people," he writes. "Near Los Angeles industries, agricultural activities, and only one or two miles from the beach. You must dig a cess-pool for your first payment; carry the 6% interest of $4.00 a month—and taxes. We require no other money payment for five whole years. You must build at least a two room cottage within a year" (GOG, p. 17). The next one hundred pages tell how the Hoags' skepticism—most particularly Pa's—turns to partisanship as they do, indeed, find their fruitful acre.

What is most impressive about Hartranft's reply is its optimism, its wholehearted endorsement of the Edenic myth, which Ma reads about as they drive into Los Angeles. "Taking a living in California," preaches the literature they have picked up along the way, "is almost as easy as the natives have it in the South Sea Islands where they gather their living from the wild trees" (GOG, p. 58). Midway through the book, a Thoreauvean sage wanders into the Hoag camp, munching carob bean and "radiating" Thoreau's doctrines of simplicity and economy. Thus inspired, the optimistic Ma takes to reading Thoreau— "through its first chapter at least" (p. 61)—and to believing that they too can survive off the land. With another family, the Hoags find their garden plot on the outskirts of Los Angeles.

And they learn "acre-culture," to live off what their gardens produce; to own pigs, not pups; to plant food-bearing trees that also have "foliage that would make a peacock stutter" (p. 105). Self-sufficiency is thus given highest priority—and government assistance is scorned.

Indeed, Hartranft's reply is as American a document as is Mitchell's—and Steinbeck's. What is particularly striking about these rebuttals is that the values endorsed are shared by Steinbeck's own migrants. The Joads, the Hoags, and the Banners all believe in hard work, in community loyalty, in family honor, in land ownership. What differs is not the values, but a belief in their ability to succeed. From the beginning of his career, Steinbeck rejected the axiom that any human, through individual efforts, is guaranteed happiness. Perhaps at some visceral level, what Mitchell and Hartranft found most subversive about Steinbeck's novel is that it radically questions the American faith in the efficacy of work. The wealthy Mitchell, the successful Taylor, and the enterprising Hartranft simply could not comprehend that worthy, energetic people could fail. Hartranft's book ends with a rather touching tribute to his faith; his Hoags, having recently read about their friends in a book (obviously *Grapes*), are heading toward Shafter to rescue them. The recent converts to the gospel of work have become its evangelists.

Sue Sanders was undoubtedly a Kern County phenomenon, the author of a small pamphlet of limited circulation, "The Real Causes of Our Migrant Problem."[35] Hers is a personal testimonial to her equally strong faith in the initiative of migrants. Neither her tract nor Hartranft's received the national attention given the others, but she deserves brief mention in order to clarify one other central tenet in the anti-Steinbeck campaign. What is intriguing about these defenses is their ambivalence toward the migrant. On the one hand, Okies were said to be far more "filthy and unenterprising" than Steinbeck had suggested. Prejudice against the southwesterners ran deep, particularly in the Central Valley. But defenses of the migrants were as common as denunciations, perhaps because, as Mitchell, Hartranft, and Sanders show, these white farm workers, unlike the Mexicans, were perceived as pioneers. They were farmers, only one generation removed from many Oklahomans who had migrated to California in the 1920s. And they exhibited early on that most admirable of American traits, the determination to make a go of it on the last frontier.

In short, Sue Sanders's tract is, like Hartranft's, a hymn to the pioneer spirit of the staunch American farmer. In mid-1939 she launched a one-woman campaign to solve California's migrant problem by proposing that the newcomers go back to Oklahoma to farm their home turf, or what was left of it. First, as she reports in her pamphlet, she toured the camps at Arvin and Shafter and confirmed the fact that these migrants were not, as she feared, shiftless. She writes: "I could be just as proud of these people as I had ever been" (*RCMP*, p. 12). So she traveled to more camps and lifted spirits by promising destitute migrants that she would, like the Wizard of Oz, help them return to the Midwest. She organized "Okie Farm Hours" at the camps and sponsored competitions with "cash prizes for the best talks on the Farm Hour on such subjects as 'How I Would Plant a Forty-Acre Farm in My Home State,' or 'My Methods of Canning Fruits and Vegetables,' or 'How I Would Make a Salad.'" With admirable naïveté, she then went to Oklahoma and asked farmers to give the migrants land. They refused. So she sadly returned to the camps and told her migrant friends that they couldn't go home again—but they could resist relief. "A country can go bankrupt in more ways than one," she concludes. "I'm not sure but that the most fatal way is by wasting the character resources of its citizens. That is exactly what is going on under the system of giving relief. We need a system of helping. Yes, by all means. But not a system that doles out charity and takes away initiative and self respect" (p. 70). Although her solution fizzled, her faith did not.

On the one hand, Sanders's and Hartranft's enthusiastic projects are ridiculous "defenses," just as Steinbeck declared. Hartranft's garden acres helped a tiny proportion of migrants who came to Los Angeles, while Sanders's visions of deportation improved spirits but temporarily. These "solutions" were Band-Aids, and the wound continued to fester. But in company with Mitchell's and Taylor's more searching analyses, these documents share an idealism that is far from ridiculous. It is staunchly American. Theirs is the faith in individual initiative. Theirs is the belief in land ownership, in the virtues of the yeoman farmer. All four demonstrated that any conscientious migrant could make it without clamoring for state aid or collective action. What Sanders discovered as she traveled among the migrants was that "They do so well with what they have. . . . They are clean and neat" and have "ingenuity in getting along with very little."[36] What was inimical to this way of thinking was the idealism of Tom Joad, a call for action as fully American as theirs, but one rooted in group, not individual, initiative. "The Battle Hymn of the Republic," which Steinbeck insisted be printed in full on the end papers of his text, calls for a collective march onward. And Steinbeck's novel marches to the same drummer. Californians attacked *The Grapes of Wrath* so viciously not only because of its language, but also because of its vision of poverty, and its attack on a system that, in fact, many agreed was flawed. These Westerners, proud and independent themselves, lambasted a book that flouted what seemed to them irrefutable American ideals.[37] The idealism of Mitchell, Taylor, Hartranft, and Sanders was, quite simply, irreconcilable with the idealism of Tom Joad.[38]

Notes

1. Steinbeck's Elusive Woman (Ditsky)

1. John Steinbeck, *The Long Valley* (New York: Viking Press, 1938). Hereinafter identified as *TLV*.

2. Robert S. Hughes, Jr., "A Form Most Congenial to His Talents: Steinbeck, the Short Story, and The Pastures of Heaven," in press, *San Jose Studies*.

3. See Mimi Reisel Gladstein, *The Indestructible Woman in Faulkner, Hemingway, and Steinbeck* (Ann Arbor, Mich.: UMI Research Press, 1986), and Bobbi Gonzales and Mimi Reisel Gladstein, "*The Wayward Bus*: Steinbeck's Misogynistic Manifesto," in *Rediscovering Steinbeck: Revisionist Views of His Art, Politics and Intellect*, ed. Cliff Lewis and Carroll Britch (Lewiston, N.Y.: Edward Mellen Press, 1989), pp. 157–73.

4. Mimi Reisel Gladstein, "Women in the Migrant Labor Movement," in press, *San Jose Studies* (1989 San Jose *The Grapes of Wrath* Conference paper).

5. Susan Shillinglaw, "'The Chrysanthemums': Steinbeck's Pygmalion," in *Steinbeck's Short Stories in "The Long Valley": Essays in Criticism*, ed. Tetsumaro Hayashi. Steinbeck Monograph Series, no. 15 (Muncie, Ind.: Steinbeck Research Institute, Ball State University, 1991), pp. 1–9.

6. See my "The Ending of *The Grapes of Wrath*: A Further Commentary," *Agora* 2 (Fall 1973): 41–50, reprinted in my *Critical Essays on Steinbeck's "The Grapes of Wrath"* (Boston: G. K. Hall & Co., 1989), pp. 116–24.

7. See my "Steinbeck's 'Slav Girl' and the Role of the Narrator in 'The Murder,'" *Steinbeck Quarterly* 22 (Summer-Fall 1989): 68–76.

8. See my "'A Kind of Play': Dramatic Elements in John Steinbeck's 'The Chrysanthemums,'" *Wascana Review* 21 (Spring 1986): 62–72.

9. I take my cue from Leslie Fiedler, "Looking Back After 50 Years," *San Jose Studies* 16 (Winter 1990): 54–64.

10. See my "The Late John Steinbeck: Dissonance in the Post-*Grapes* Era," *San Jose Studies* 18 (Winter 1992): 20–32.

11. In this connection, an anecdote from recent experience seems appropriate. In October 1989 in Moscow, when Robert DeMott addressed the Moscow Writers' Union, he tried to save some time by handing a passage from *Working Days* over to our toothsome translator for direct translation into Russian. The passage had to do with the difficulty of coming to an end of the creative process. Unfortunately, due to unknown differences between Russian and English idioms, the translation began to seem to allude to other sorts of coming not unknown in English as well. In short, the audience was soon guffawing and tittering over what seemed to be Steinbeck's inability to achieve sexual satisfaction, when, in fact, simply finishing *The Grapes of Wrath* was all that was on his mind. Or was it? If the manuscript of *The Grapes of Wrath* were to have appeared to its progenitor veiled in nothing more substantial than a Freudian slip, should we be surprised?

12. Jocelyn Roberts in an unpublished paper on *The Winter of Our Discontent*.

13. Beth Everest and Judy Wedeles, "The Neglected Rib: Women in *East of Eden*," *Steinbeck Quarterly* 21 (Winter-Spring 1988): 13–23.

14. John Steinbeck, *Your Only Weapon Is Your Work*, ed. Robert DeMott (San Jose, Calif.: Steinbeck Research Center, 1985), p. 4.

15. John Steinbeck, *Journal of a Novel: The "East of Eden" Letters* (New York: Viking Press, 1969), p. 179.

16. Ibid., p. 10.

17. Ibid., p. 11.

2. After *The Grapes of Wrath* (DeMott)

1. On an otherwise bleak trip to New York in late April 1949, Steinbeck also visited Wanda. On the flight home he wrote two notes to her. The first, postmarked May 5, says, "I was very happy and you were my happiness"; the second, also postmarked that day, says, "I remember every minute and love all of them. And don't think your present is not deeply, deeply appreciated. Good night darling." Both are signed "J." Courtesy of the Steinbeck Research Center, Wahlquist Library, San Jose State University, San Jose, Calif. For more on these letters, see Dana Rubin, "SJS Buys 31 Steinbeck Letters," *San Jose Mercury News*, October 26, 1985, pp. 1B, 2B; and Carol Ryan, "University Buys Steinbeck's 'Dark Night' Letters," *Salinas Californian*, October 26, 1985, pp. 1, 12.

2. John Ditsky, "John Steinbeck—Yesterday, Today, and Tomorrow," *Steinbeck Quarterly* 23 (Winter-Spring 1990): 12.

3. Elaine Steinbeck and Robert Wallsten, eds., *Steinbeck: A Life in Letters* (New York: Viking Press, 1975), p. 220. Hereinafter identified as *SLL*.

4. Jackson J. Benson, *The True Adventures of John Steinbeck, Writer* (New York: Viking Press, 1984), pp. 402–5, 494–96, 618–22. Hereinafter identified as *TAJS*.

5. John Steinbeck, *Working Days: The Journal of "The Grapes of Wrath": 1938–1941*, ed. Robert DeMott (New York: Viking Press, 1989), pp. 102–3. Hereinafter identified as *WD*.

6. My information about the location of Steinbeck's poetry manuscript comes from several sources: a Black Sun Books catalog; a brief note by Kiyoshi Nakayama, "Steinbeck's Love Poems," in *The John Steinbeck Society of Japan Newsletter 7* (May 1984): 13; a letter written to me on August 17, 1984, by Mary Jean S. Gamble, Steinbeck Librarian, John Steinbeck Library, Salinas, Calif.; a telephone conversation with Steinbeck's eldest son, Thomas, on October 3, 1985; and the introduction by Terry Halladay to Gwyn Steinbeck's autobiography, documented in the following note.

7. Terry Grant Halladay, "'The Closest Witness': The Autobiographical Reminiscences of Gwyndolyn Conger Steinbeck." M.A. thesis, Stephen F. Austin University, 1979. Hereinafter identified as "CW." The bulk of this 330-page work is a rendering of Gwyn's unfinished and frequently interrupted oral reminiscences and interviews, recorded with Douglas Brown between March and May of 1971. Halladay edited the jumbled and contradictory (but always revealing) material into a relatively coherent narrative and added appropriate introductory statements, annotations, and notes. The thesis is available on demand from University Microfilms, 300 North Zeeb Road, Ann Arbor, MI 48106 (order number 1313147). Recently, I learned that Thom Steinbeck and John Steinbeck IV planned to publish a separate edition of their father's poems to their mother. Catalogue Four (1990) of MacDonnell's Rare Books (Austin, Tex.) lists for sale (at $250.00): "LOVE POEMS TO GWYN CONGER STEINBECK. Austin, 1978. Unpublished typescript. 27pp. A collection of twenty-five poems with mock-up of title page and colophon, prepared for private publication for members of the Steinbeck family, but apparently never published" (entry 453).

8. John Steinbeck, *The Log from the Sea of Cortez* (New York: Viking Press, 1951), p. xxxix. Hereinafter identified as *Log*.

9. John Steinbeck, *Letters to Elizabeth: A Selection of Letters from John Steinbeck to Elizabeth Otis*, ed. Florian J. Shasky and Susan F. Riggs (San Francisco: The Book Club of California, 1978), pp. 17–18. Hereinafter identified as *LTE*.

10. Unpublished letter to Annie Laurie Williams (February 7, 1949), courtesy of the Department of Special Collections, Butler Library, Columbia University, New York.

11. Mimi Reisel Gladstein, *The Indestructible Woman in Faulkner, Hemingway, and Steinbeck* (Ann Arbor, Mich.: UMI Research Press, 1986), pp. 75–100.

12. Some intriguing psycho-biographical implications of Steinbeck's sexual/textual transference are noted in Kenneth S. Lynn's review of *Working Days* in the August 1989 issue of *American Spectator*, pp. 41–42.

13. Unpublished letter (1941), courtesy of Clifton Waller Barrett Library, University of Virginia Library, Charlottesville, Va.

14. Susan Shillinglaw is working on a full-length biography of Carol. See her editor's report on the recent acquisition of Carol's library and papers in the *Steinbeck Newsletter* 2 (Fall 1988): 1–2, the journal of San Jose State University's Steinbeck Research Center.

3. Looking at Lisa (Werlock)

1. Elaine Steinbeck and Robert Wallsten, eds., *Steinbeck: A Life in Letters* (New York: Viking Press, 1975), pp. 105–6.

2. See, for example, Jackson J. Benson and Ann Loftis, "John Steinbeck and Farm Labor Unionization: The Background of *In Dubious Battle*," *American Literature* 52 (May 1980): 196–97; Peter Lisca, *John Steinbeck: Nature and Myth* (New York: Thomas Y. Crowell, 1975), p. 68; John L. Gribben, "Steinbeck's *East of Eden* and Milton's *Paradise Lost*: A Discussion of 'Timshel,'" in *Steinbeck's Literary Dimension: A Guide to Comparative Studies*, ed. Tetsumaro Hayashi (Metuchen, N.J.: Scarecrow Press, 1973), p. 99; Joseph Fontenrose, *John Steinbeck: An Introduction and Interpretation* (New York: Holt, Rinehart and Winston, 1963), p. 46; John H. Timmerman, *John Steinbeck's Fiction: The Aesthetics of the Road Taken* (Norman: University of Oklahoma Press, 1986), p. 88; Allen

Shepherd, "On the Dubiousness of Steinbeck's *In Dubious Battle*," *Notes on Modern American Literature* 2 (1978): Item 19; Warren French, *John Steinbeck* (New York: Twayne Publishers, 1961), p. 62; Anthony F. R. Palmieri, "*In Dubious Battle*: A Portrait in Pessimism," *Artes Liberales* 3 (1976): 69; Barry W. Sarchett, "*In Dubious Battle*: A Revaluation," *Steinbeck Quarterly* 13 (Summer-Fall 1980): 88; Louis Owens, *John Steinbeck's Re-Vision of America* (Athens: University of Georgia Press, 1985), p. 98; Jerry W. Wilson, "*In Dubious Battle*: Engagement in Collectivity," *Steinbeck Quarterly* 13 (Winter-Spring 1980): 37.

3. Benson and Loftis, "Steinbeck and Farm Labor," p. 196.

4. Peter Lisca, *The Wide World of John Steinbeck* (New Brunswick, N.J.: Rutgers University Press, 1958), p. 206.

5. Benson and Loftis, "Steinbeck and Farm Labor," pp. 190–223.

6. Mimi Reisel Gladstein, *The Indestructible Woman in Faulkner, Hemingway, and Steinbeck* (Ann Arbor, Mich.: UMI Research Press, 1986), pp. 90–91.

7. Benson and Loftis, "Steinbeck and Farm Labor," p. 214.

8. Jackson J. Benson, *The True Adventures of John Steinbeck, Writer* (New York: Viking Press, 1984), p. 308.

9. Benson and Loftis, "Steinbeck and Farm Labor," p. 219.

10. Ibid., p. 210.

11. Benson, *The True Adventures*, p. 239.

12. Quoted in Richard Astro, *John Steinbeck and Edward F. Ricketts: The Shaping of a Novelist* (Minneapolis: University of Minnesota Press, 1973), p. 133.

13. Warren Motley, "From Patriarchy to Matriarchy: Ma Joad's Role in *The Grapes of Wrath*," *American Literature* 54 (October 1982): 398–99.

14. Robert Briffault, *The Mothers: The Matriarchal Theory of Social Origins* (New York: Grosset and Dunlop, 1931), p. 434.

15. Ibid.

16. Benson, *The True Adventures*, p. 223.

17. John Steinbeck, *In Dubious Battle* (1936; New York: Bantam,

1963), p. 233. Subsequent references are to this edition and are identified as *IDB*.

18. Gladstein, *Indestructible Woman*, p. 26.

19. Ibid., p. 28.

20. Ibid., p. 27.

21. Ibid., p. 31.

22. French, *John Steinbeck*, p. 62.

23. Gladstein, *Indestructible Woman*, p. 27.

24. Timmerman, *John Steinbeck's Fiction*, p. 85.

25. Anthony F. R. Palmieri, "Portrait in Pessimism," p. 65.

26. John Milton, *Paradise Lost*, in *John Milton: Complete Poems and Major Prose*, ed. Merritt Y. Hughes (Indianapolis: Odyssey Press, 1957), Book IX, line 625, p. 393.

27. Carol Gilligan, *In a Different Voice: Psychological Theory and Women's Development* (Cambridge: Harvard University Press, 1982), p. 2.

28. Ibid.

29. Howard Levant, "The Unity of *In Dubious Battle*: Violence and Dehumanization," in *Steinbeck: A Collection of Critical Essays*, ed. Robert Murray Davis (Englewood Cliffs, N.J.: Prentice-Hall, 1972), p. 59.

30. Ibid.

31. Quoted in Gilligan, *Different Voice*, p. 17.

32. Ibid., p. 2.

33. Steinbeck and Wallsten, *Steinbeck: A Life in Letters*, p. 98.

34. Gladstein, *Indestructible Woman*, pp. 110–11.

35. Ibid., p. 105.

4. Dialogic Tension (Hadella)

1. Jackson J. Benson, *The True Adventures of John Steinbeck, Writer* (New York: Viking Press, 1984), p. 363. Benson states that the play was "a success, a distinct hit of the season, an award-winner, and ran for 207 performances at the Music Box Theatre."

2. Elaine Steinbeck and Robert Wallsten, eds., *Steinbeck: A Life in Letters* (New York: Viking Press, 1975), p. 154. Hereinafter identified as *SLL*.

3. Mikhail Bakhtin, *The Dialogic Imagination: Four Essays by M. M. Bakhtin*, trans. Caryl Emerson, ed. Michael Holquist (Austin: University of Texas Press, 1981), pp. 314–15.

4. Charles I. Schuster, "Mikhail Bakhtin as Rhetorical Theorist," *College English* 47 (October 1985): 595.

5. Bakhtin, *Dialogic Imagination*, p. 293.

6. John Steinbeck, *Of Mice and Men*, in *Famous American Plays of the 1930s*, ed. Harold Clurman (New York: Dell, 1974), p. 350. Subsequent references are to this edition and are identified as *OMM*.

7. Louis Owens, *John Steinbeck's Re-Vision of America* (Athens: University of Georgia Press, 1985), p. 100.

8. "Men, Mice and Mr. Steinbeck," *New York Times*, December 5, 1937, reprinted in Thomas Fensch, ed., *Conversations with John Steinbeck* (Jackson: University Press of Mississippi, 1988), p. 9.

9. Owens, *Steinbeck's Re-Vision*, p. 103.

10. Peter Lisca, *The Wide World of John Steinbeck* (1958; New York: Gordian Press, 1981), p. 138. Page references are to this edition.

11. Ibid.

12. Mark Spilka, "Of George and Lennie and Curley's Wife: Sweet Violence in Steinbeck's Eden," *Modern Fiction Studies* 20 (Summer 1974): 174.

13. Ibid.

14. Howard Levant, *The Novels of John Steinbeck: A Critical Study* (Columbia: University of Missouri Press, 1974), p. 138.

15. Sandra Beatty, "Steinbeck's Play-Women: A Study of the Female Presence in *Of Mice and Men, Burning Bright, The Moon Is Down*, and *Viva Zapata!*" in *Steinbeck's Women: Essays in Criticism*, ed. Tetsumaro Hayashi, Steinbeck Monograph Series, no. 9 (Muncie, Ind.: Steinbeck Society of America, Ball State University, 1979), p. 7.

16. Ibid., p. 8.

17. Owens, *Steinbeck's Re-Vision*, p. 103.

18. Ibid.

5. Writing "in Costume" (Owens)

1. Stephen J. Greenblatt, "Shakespeare and the Exorcists," in *Contemporary Literary Criticism: Literary and Cultural Studies*, ed. Robert Con Davis and Ronald Schleifer (New York: Longman, 1989), p. 429.

2. Carlos Bulosan, "My Education," in *If You Want to Know What We Are: A Carlos Bulosan Reader*, ed. E. San Juan, Jr. (Minneapolis: West End Press, 1983), p. 19.

3. Ibid.

4. Elaine Steinbeck and Robert Wallsten, eds., *Steinbeck: A Life in Letters* (New York: Viking Press, 1975), p. 87. Hereinafter identified as *SLL*.

5. Carlos Bulosan, *America Is in the Heart: A Personal History 1946* (Seattle: University of Washington Press, 1973). Hereinafter identified as *AIH*.

6. John Steinbeck, *In Dubious Battle* (1936; New York: Bantam, 1972), p. 6. Subsequent references are to this edition and are identified as *IDB*.

7. Quoted in Jackson J. Benson, *The True Adventures of John Steinbeck, Writer* (New York: Viking Press, 1984), p. 325.

8. Ibid., p. 315.

9. Jackson J. Benson and Anne Loftis, "John Steinbeck and Farm Labor Unionization: The Background of *In Dubious Battle*," *American Literature* 52 (May 1980): 210.

10. Ibid., p. 215.

11. Carey McWilliams, *Factories in the Fields: The Story of Migratory Farm Labor in California* (Boston: Little, Brown and Co., 1939), p. 133.

12. Ibid., p. 237.

13. Ibid., p. 246.

14. Benson, *The True Adventures*, p. 316.

15. McWilliams, *Factories*, p. 246.

16. Vicki L. Ruiz, *Cannery Women, Cannery Lives: Mexican Women, Unionization, and the California Food Processing Industry, 1930–50* (Albuquerque: University of New Mexico Press, 1987), p. 8.

17. Benson, *The True Adventures*, p. 303.

18. Mikhail Bakhtin, "Discourse in the Novel," in *The Dialogic Imagination: Four Essays by M. M. Bakhtin*, ed. Michael Holquist, trans. Caryl Emerson and Michael Holquist (Austin: University of Texas Press, 1981), p. 346.

19. Ibid., p. 324.

20. Ibid., p. 342.

21. Ibid.

22. Ibid.

23. Ibid., p. 430.

24. McWilliams, *Factories*, p. 118.

25. Ibid., p. 223.

26. Benson and Loftis, "John Steinbeck and Farm Labor," p. 223.

27. Benson, *The True Adventures*, p. 304.

28. Hector Galan and David Marash, *New Harvest, Old Shame*, produced and directed by Hector Galan, "Frontline," WGBH-TV, April 17, 1990.

6. Sharing Creation (Tammaro)

1. James D. Hart, "Proletarian Literature," in *The Oxford Companion to American Literature* (New York: Oxford University Press, 1983), pp. 610–11.

2. Frederick J. Hoffman, "Aesthetics of the Proletarian Novel," in *Proletarian Writers of the Thirties*, ed. David Madden (Carbondale: Southern Illinois University Press, 1968), p. 184.

3. Ibid.

4. Ibid.

5. Ibid., p. 189.

6. Nicholas Coles, "Democratizing Literature: Issues in Teaching Working-Class Literature," *College English* 48 (November 1986): 667.

7. Ibid., p. 669.

8. Upton Sinclair, *The Jungle* (Urbana: University of Illinois Press, 1988), p. ix.

9. Louis Owens, *Steinbeck's Re-Vision of America* (Athens: University of Georgia Press, 1985), p. 90.

10. Warren French, *John Steinbeck*, 2d ed. (Indianapolis: Bobbs-Merrill, 1975), p. 76.

11. Hoffman, "Proletarian Novel," p. 193.

12. Ibid., p. 189.

13. Ibid., p. 193.

14. Harold Bloom, ed., *John Steinbeck: Modern Critical Views* (New York: Chelsea House, 1987), p. 1.

15. Coles, "Democratizing Literature," p. 665.

16. Jackson J. Benson, *The True Adventures of John Steinbeck, Writer* (New York: Viking Press, 1984), p. 41.

17. Louis Owens raises a related and interesting point in his essay "Writing 'in Costume': The Missing Voices of *In Dubious Battle*." He writes that Steinbeck's aesthetic architecture for *In Dubious Battle*, while creating a highly successful and popular novel, simultaneously and inadvertently silences those minority voices—namely Mexican and Filipino workers—who figure so prominently in the historical, social, political, and economic reality of the novel but are obviously absent from the novel itself. The appropriation of their story without novelistic representation further marginalizes their voices and experiences. The degree to which *In Dubious Battle* is omitted from curricula because of this oversight and inaccuracy is difficult to gauge. If the novel is discussed in the hermetically sealed world of New Criticism, the issue is a moot point. However, dis-

cussed in a larger, sociopolitical context, the novel does open itself to this charge. Owens would not deny Steinbeck's right to manipulate the raw materials for his fiction, for *In Dubious Battle* is, ultimately, a fiction, he believes. But what Owens convincingly suggests is an irony: in his desire to write an objective, nonjudgmental book, Steinbeck—confusing a "dramatic method" with "impossible authorial objectivity"—wrote a highly personal and subjective novel.

18. Coles, "Democratizing Literature," p. 666.

19. Ibid., p. 677.

20. Janice Castro, "Labor Draws an Empty Gun," *Time*, March 26, 1990, p. 57.

7. Reflections of Doc (Fensch)

1. Telephone interview with Pauline Pearson, May 4, 1990.

2. Richard Astro, *John Steinbeck and Edward F. Ricketts: The Shaping of a Novelist* (Minneapolis: University of Minnesota Press, 1973), p. 4.

3. Ibid., p. 122.

4. Ibid., p. 152.

5. Ibid., p. 184.

6. Ibid., p. 113.

7. Thomas K. Whipple, "Steinbeck: Through a Glass though Brightly," *New Republic* 90 (October 12, 1938): 274–75; quoted in Astro, *Steinbeck and Ricketts*, p. 106.

8. John Steinbeck, *Of Mice and Men* (New York: Covici-Friede, 1937), pp. 61–62.

9. Astro, *Steinbeck and Ricketts*, p. 106.

10. Jackson J. Benson, *The True Adventures of John Steinbeck, Writer* (New York: Viking Press, 1984), p. 327.

11. Astro, *Steinbeck and Ricketts*, p. 107.

8. Tell Again, George (Morsberger)

1. John Steinbeck, *Burning Bright, a Play in Story Form* (New York: Bantam Books, 1951), p. 1.

2. Ibid., pp. 1–2.

3. Ibid., p. 3.

4. Elaine Steinbeck and Robert Wallsten, eds., *Steinbeck: A Life in Letters* (New York: Viking Press, 1975), p. 132.

5. Glenn Collins, "Staging a 'Grapes' of Dust, Fog, Fire and Blood," *New York Times*, April 3, 1990, p. C20.

6. Margaret Shedd, "*Of Mice and Men*," *Theatre Arts Monthly* 21 (October 1937): 775.

7. Warren French, "The First Theatrical Production of Steinbeck's *Of Mice and Men*," *American Literature* 36 (January 1965): 525–27.

8. Ibid., p. 525.

9. Steinbeck, *Burning Bright*, p. 1.

10. French, "First Theatrical Production," p. 525.

11. Shedd, "*Of Mice*," p. 775.

12. Ibid., p. 780.

13. Jackson J. Benson, *The True Adventures of John Steinbeck, Writer* (New York: Viking Press, 1984), p. 351.

14. Steinbeck and Wallsten, *Steinbeck: A Life in Letters*, p. 136.

15. Ibid., p. 141.

16. Ibid., p. 136.

17. John Steinbeck, *Of Mice and Men, Play*, in *20 Best Plays of the Modern American Theatre*, ed. John Gassner (New York: Crown, 1939), p. 655.

18. Ibid., p. 656.

19. Ibid., p. 666.

20. Ibid., p. 672.

21. Steinbeck and Wallsten, *Steinbeck: A Life in Letters*, p. 137.

22. Ibid., p. 141.

23. Brooks Atkinson, "Review of *Of Mice and Men*," *New York Times*, November 24, 1937, 20:5.

24. Atkinson, "Episode in the Lower Depths," *New York Times*, December 12, 1937, XI:3:1.

25. "*Of Mice and Men* Wins Critics Prize," *New York Times*, April 19, 1938, p. 23.

26. George Jean Nathan, "Theater," *Scribner's Magazine* 103 (February 1938), p. 70.

27. Charles Morgan, "Steinbeck in London," *New York Times*, April 30, 1939, XI:3:5.

28. Louis Calta, "Movie of the Week: *Of Mice and Men*," *New York Times*, December 5, 1958, 38:1.

29. Martin Bernheimer, "Opera Review," *Los Angeles Times*, March 18, 1974, sec. IV, p. 1.

30. Nathan, "Theater," p. 70.

31. Benson, *The True Adventures*, p. 372.

32. Charles Higham and Joel Greenberg, "Lewis Milestone," in *The Celluloid Muse: Hollywood Directors Speak* (New York: Viking Press, 1972), p. 158.

33. Aaron Copland and Vivian Perlis, *Copland 1900 through 1942* (New York: St. Martin's/Marek, 1984), p. 297.

34. Ibid., p. 298.

35. Arnold Dobrin, *Aaron Copland: His Life and Times* (New York: Thomas Y. Crowell, 1967), p. 146.

36. Copland and Perlis, *Copland*, p. 242.

37. Dobrin, *Aaron Copland*, p. 152.

38. Copland and Perlis, *Copland*, p. 298.

39. Julia Smith, *Aaron Copland* (New York: E. P. Dutton, 1955), p. 202.

40. "Movie of the Week: *Of Mice and Men*," *Life* 8 (January 8, 1940), p. 42.

41. William K. Everson, *The Films of Hal Roach* (Greenwich, Conn.: Museum of Modern Art, New York, 1971), pp. 75, 77.

42. Steven Winn, "*Of Mice and Men* Brings Sinise Full Circle," *San Francisco Chronicle*, October 10, 1992, sec. C, p. 5.

43. Ibid.

44. Ibid.

45. Peter Rainer, "Mice and Men, '92 Edition, Squeaks By," *Los Angeles Times*, October 2, 1992, sec. C, p. 5.

46. Vincent Canby, "New Facets Highlighted in a Classic," *New York Times*, October 2, 1992, sec. C, p. 5.

9. Steinbeck and the Eternal Immigrant (Gladstein)

1. Leslie Fiedler, "Looking Back After 50 Years," *San Jose Studies* 16 (Winter 1990): 64.

2. Harold Bloom, ed., *John Steinbeck's "The Grapes of Wrath"* (New York: Chelsea House, 1988), p. 5.

3. Stephen Schaefer, "New *Grapes* Still Bears Fruit," *USA Today*, March 23, 1990, p. 4D.

4. David Patrick Stearns, "Steppenwolf's Gritty Honesty Dazzles in Clear, Classic Style," *USA Today*, March 23, 1990, p. 4D.

5. Ibid.

6. Mimi Kramer, "Tender Grapes," *New Yorker*, April 2, 1990, pp. 87–88.

7. Alan Brinkley, "Why Steinbeck's Okies Speak to Us Today," *New York Times*, March 18, 1990, sec. 2, p. 13.

8. Elaine Steinbeck and Robert Wallsten, eds., *Steinbeck: A Life in Letters* (New York: Viking Press, 1975), pp. 178–79.

9. John Steinbeck, *The Harvest Gypsies* (1936; Berkeley, Calif.: Heyday Books, 1988), p. 62.

10. Ibid., p. xi.

11. John Steinbeck, *The Grapes of Wrath* (New York: Viking Press, 1939), p. 322. Hereinafter identified as *GOW*.

12. I consulted a number of books in order to establish the universal character of the immigrant experience. Some of these works are cited in the text, but others are not because of the limited nature of my presentation. Among the works consulted but not cited are: Thomas D. Boswell and James R. Curtis, *The Cuban-American*

Experience (Totawa, N.J.: Rowman & Allanheld Publishers, 1984); Francesco Cordasco and Eugene Bucchioni, *The Puerto Rican Experience* (Totawa, N.J.: Rowman & Littlefield, 1973); Thomas Hammar, ed., *European Immigration Policy: A Comparative Study* (Cambridge: Cambridge University Press, 1985); Patrick J. Gallo, *Ethnic Alienation: The Italian-Americans* (Teaneck, N.J.: Fairleigh Dickinson University Press, 1974); R. M. MacIver, ed., *Group Relations and Antagonisms* (New York: Institute for Religious Studies and Harper & Brothers, 1944); Oscar Handlin, *Immigration as a Factor in American History* (Englewood Cliffs, N.J.: Prentice-Hall, 1959); Thomas H. Holloway, *Immigrants on the Land* (Chapel Hill: University of North Carolina Press, 1980); Woo Moo Hurh and Kwang Chung Kim, *Korean Immigrants in America* (Teaneck, N.J.: Fairleigh Dickinson University Press, 1984); Hans Christiann Buechler and Judith-Maria Buechler, eds., *Migrants in Europe* (Westport, Conn.: Greenwood Press, 1987); Constantine M. Panunzio, *The Soul of an Immigrant* (New York: Arno Press and *New York Times*, 1969); Sherman C. Bezalel, *The Jew within American Society* (Detroit: Wayne State University Press, 1961); Carl Solberg, *Immigration and Nationalism: Argentina and Chile, 1890–1914* (Austin: University of Texas Press, 1970); Barbara Miller Solomon, *Ancestors and Immigrants* (Cambridge: Harvard University Press, 1956).

13. Michael A. Musmanno, *The Story of the Italians in America* (Garden City, N.Y.: Doubleday, 1965), p. 6.

14. Vincent N. Parrillo, *Strangers to These Shores: Race and Ethnic Relations in the United States,* 2d ed. (New York: John Wiley & Sons, 1985), pp. 64–65. Parrillo defines ethnophaulism as "the language of prejudice, the verbal picture of a negative stereotype."

15. George Lynn Cross, *Presidents Can't Punt* (Norman: University of Oklahoma Press, 1977), p. 7.

16. John Rechy, "El Paso del Norte," in *New Writing in the USA,* ed. Donald Allen and Robert Creeley (Middlesex, England: Penguin Books, 1967), p. 211.

17. Ronald L. Goldfarb, *Migrant Farm Workers: A Caste of Despair* (Ames: Iowa State University Press, 1981), p. 40.

18. Brent Ashabrenner, *Dark Harvest: Migrant Farm Workers in America* (New York: Dodd, Mead & Co., 1985).

19. James N. Gregory, *American Exodus: The Dust Bowl Migration and Okie Culture in California* (New York: Oxford University Press, 1989).

10. California Answers (Shillinglaw)

1. Tom Cameron, "*The Grapes of Wrath* Author Guards Self from Threats at Moody Gulch," *Los Angeles Times*, July 9, 1939, pp. 1–2.

2. James N. Gregory, *American Exodus: The Dust Bowl Migration and Okie Culture in California* (New York: Oxford University Press, 1989), p. 88.

3. Walter J. Stein, *California and the Dust Bowl Migration* (Westport, Conn.: Greenwood Press, 1973), p. 97. Gregory calls this stage of reaction "the second anti-migrant campaign" (*American Exodus*, p. 88). Since the mid-1930s, valley residents had viewed the Southwestern migrants with increasing disdain, complaining of their poverty and strange ways and, more pointedly, of their need for schooling and health care, which had sent taxes soaring. The crisis in the migrant problem came in 1938, when the second Agricultural Adjustment Act set new controls for California cotton, resulting in fewer acres planted and fewer jobs for migrants.

4. Elsie Robinson, "The Truth About California: Red Ousters Urged as State's Only Solution to End Migrant Evil," *San Francisco Examiner* ["March of Events" section], January 14, 1940, p. 1.

5. See George Thomas Miron, "The Truth About John Steinbeck and the Migrants" (Los Angeles, 1939), p. 4, Bancroft Library, University of California, Berkeley; and John E. Pickett, "Termites Steinbeck and McWilliams," *Pacific Rural Press*, July 29, 1939.

6. Interview with Richard Criley, June 21, 1990.

7. Similarities between the two are intriguing. Like Steinbeck, Ruth Comfort Mitchell loved dogs, the outdoors, and music, believing that of all the arts, "music is the only art that restores us to ourselves." While still a teenager, she, too, devoted her time to writing; her first poem, "To Los Gatos," was published in the local paper when she was thirteen, and at nineteen she had launched a successful career as a writer for vaudeville. Also like Steinbeck, she refused to see her most popular productions during their New York runs. When Mitchell and her husband built a house in Los Gatos in 1916, she, like Steinbeck, built a study "with the floor space of a postcard" where she wrote for four to twelve hours daily. See Stella Haverland, "Ruth Comfort Mitchell," pp. 122–26, Ruth Comfort Mitchell Papers, San Jose Public Library.

8. *Pittsburgh Dispatch*, August 29, 1909.

9. *Los Angeles Times Sun*, Ruth Comfort Mitchell Papers, San Jose Public Library.

10. Sanborn Young owned the two thousand-acre Riverdale Ranch, a dairy ranch near Fresno in the San Joaquin Valley; he was also part owner of the New Idria quicksilver mine in San Benito County. He took his new wife to his dairy farm after their marriage in 1914; it was during her few years on that farm and in subsequent visits that she gained her perspective on California's labor problems.

A senator from 1924 to 1928 and 1930 to 1932, Young became a prominent voice in state politics, largely through his support of narcotics control. In 1931 he and Mitchell attended an international conference on narcotics in Geneva (May 27–July 13), and nine years later he remained a chief spokesman for this issue, claiming that "California has between 3000 and 6000 narcotics addicts, and addiction to marijuana—Indian hemp—is rapidly increasing" (*Los Gatos Times*, March 10, 1939, p. 3). Less highly publicized was his support for the Associated Farmers and, in all likelihood, for the CCA.

11. Tim Kappel, "Trampling Out the Vineyards—Kern County's Ban on *The Grapes of Wrath*," *California History* 61 (Fall 1982): 212.

12. "Pro America Gives 'Other Side' of Story to Migrant Problems," *Los Gatos Times*, August 25, 1939, p. 1.

13. *Fresno Bee*, a report of a meeting on the status of California farm workers, August 23, 1939.

14. Mitchell repeatedly denied that her novel was written in response to Steinbeck's. In a letter to a friend, JHJ, she says: "Will you please PLEASE emphasize the fact—as you so kindly did once before—that it wasn't an 'answer' or 'challenge to GRAPES OF WRATH,' that it was planned, plotted, named before I read G-O-W, that I yield to no one in my admiration for the genius of John Steinbeck? . . . I sent JS a copy from a 'Los Gatos wild cat to a literary lion,' and he sent me IN DUBIOUS BATTLE, which is my favorite, altho' MICE AND MEN is a gorgeous pattern." (This was probably written May 8, 1940.) Mitchell Papers, Bancroft Library, University of California, Berkeley.

Mitchell's protests notwithstanding, her book played a part in the Associated Farmers' campaign. Mitchell was "preparing to give California's answer as principal speaker at the banquet on December 7 which opens the two-day convention of the Associated Farmers of California at Stockton" ("Ruth Comfort Mitchell to Address Meeting of Associated Farmers," *Los Gatos Times*, November 24, 1939, p. 5). She spoke on "her version of 'The Grapes of Wrath'" ("Noted Authoress Answers Charges of Novel, Defends Migrants," *Stockton Record*, December 8, 1939, pp. 1, 21). (See also "Writer to Discuss Steinbeck Book Before Farmers Meet," *Stockton Record*, December 5, 1939, p. 13.)

Furthermore, records indicate that she did indeed write in response to Steinbeck's text. The first notice of Mitchell's book in the Los Gatos paper is June 30, 1939—nearly three months after publication of *Grapes*. The contract for *Of Human Kindness* was not signed until October 19, 1939, and the book was not published until May 1940. (See also *New Republic* 103 [September 2, 1940], p. 305, where Carey McWilliams shows that Mitchell publicly responded to Steinbeck on many occasions.)

15. Philip Bancroft, "The Farmer and the Communists," [San Francisco] *Daily Commercial News,* April 29, 30, 1935.

16. Ruth Comfort Mitchell, *Of Human Kindness* (New York: D. Appleton-Century Co., 1940), p. 5. Hereinafter identified as *OHK.*

17. Miron, "Truth about Steinbeck," p. 21.

18. Labor historian Anne Loftis pointed out this possible parallel to me. Stein, however, sees the "Black Widow" as Steinbeck himself.

19. Bancroft, "Farmer and Communists," p. 7.

20. Frank J. Taylor, "One Story Leads to Another," Frank Taylor Papers, Department of Special Collections, Stanford University Libraries.

21. See "The Flowers and the Bees," *Collier's* (September 9, 1939); "Color from California: More than Half the World's Supply of Flower Seeds Come from This State," *California—Magazine of Pacific Business* (November 1939); "Mr. Gump—of Gump's: A Romance of Treasure Trove in San Francisco," *California—Magazine of Pacific Business* (April 1937); "Soil-less Crops," *Country Home* (September 1936), pp. 18–19; "Mickey Mouse—Merchant: A Personality Sketch of a Native Son and California's No. 1 Merchandiser," *California—Magazine of Pacific Business* (March 1937); "What Has Disney Got that We Haven't," *Commentator* (October 1937). I wish to thank Frank J. Taylor's son, Robert Taylor, for generously showing me scrapbooks of articles written by his father.

22. Frank J. Taylor, "The Merritt System," *Commentator* (November 1938), pp. 84–87. (The article was reprinted in *Reader's Digest* 35 [February 1939], pp. 104–6. Frank Taylor Papers, Department of Special Collections, Stanford University Libraries.)

23. Frank J. Taylor, "Teague of California," *Country Home* (November 1935), p. 36.

24. Taylor, "The Right to Harvest," *Country Gentleman* (October 1937), p. 8.

25. Taylor, "Labor on Wheels," *Country Gentleman* (July 1938), p. 12.

26. Taylor, "The Right to Harvest," p. 8.

27. Taylor, "Green Gold and Tear Gas: What Really Happened in the Salinas Lettuce Strike," *California—Magazine of Pacific Business* (November 1936), p. 18.

28. Taylor, "The Story Behind 'The Many Californias—An Armchair Travelogue'—*R.D.*, January 1952." Frank Taylor Papers, Department of Special Collections, Stanford University Libraries.

29. Taylor, "California's *Grapes of Wrath*," *Forum* 102 (November 1939): p. 232. Hereinafter identified as "CGOW."

30. Stein, *California and Migration*, p. 41.

31. Gregory, *American Exodus*, pp. 19–35.

32. Maud O. Bartlett, "Wrath on Both Sides," *Forum* 103 (January 1940): p. 24.

33. Marshall V. Hartranft, *Grapes of Gladness: California's Refreshing and Inspiring Answer to John Steinbeck's "Grapes of Wrath"* (Los Angeles: DeVorss and Co., 1939), p. 1. Hereinafter identified as *GOG*.

34. John Steven McGroarty, *History of Los Angeles County* (Chicago: American Historical Society, 1923), p. 767.

35. Sue Sanders, "The Real Causes of Our Migrant Problem" (1940). I wish to thank John Walden of the Kern County Library for his help with material relating to Sue Sanders and the film "The Plums of Plenty" (see below).

36. Mae Saunders, "Migrants Regard Sue Sanders as True Friend," *Bakersfield Californian*, October 21, 1939, pp. 12, 19.

37. One other response to *Grapes* should be mentioned, a short film, now lost, entitled "The Plums of Plenty." Perhaps because of its catchy title, this work is often referred to but seldom identified. In "Steinbeck and the Migrants: A Study of *The Grapes of Wrath*," an M.A. thesis written by John Schamberger at the University of Colorado in 1960, the film's history is summarized: "Emory Gay Hoffman, the manager of the Kern County Chamber of Commerce at the time of publication of *The Grapes of Wrath*, wrote a short story entitled 'Plums of Plenty' in answer to Steinbeck's novel. According to Hoffman, the six-thousand-word draft of 'Plums of Plenty' was

lost which precluded its publication. However, a 'movie short' was published from the notes and . . . much of the colored motion picture was used by the old Kern County Chamber of Commerce and 'News of the Day,' a Movie Tone release. Hoffman stated that William B. Camp had sponsored the authorship of his book and the motion picture" (pp. 64–65).

38. On February 11, 1952, Steinbeck gave an interview for the Voice of America, and he was asked if he saw "any changes in the conditions since the time that you were there [in the Dust Bowl] during the research for your novel?" Steinbeck's reply provides a fitting footnote to *Grapes* and to this article: "Oh yes. I found a great many changes. . . . When I wrote *The Grapes of Wrath* I was filled naturally with certain anger and certain anger at people who were doing injustices to other people, or so I thought. I realize now that everyone was caught in the same trap." In California, the migrants "met a people who were terrified, for number one, of the depression and were horrified at the idea that great numbers of indigent people were being poured on them, to be taken care of. They could only be taken care of by taxation, taxes were already high and there wasn't much money about. They reacted perfectly normally, they became angry. When you become angry you fight what you are angry at. They were angry at these newcomers. Gradually through government agency, through the work of private citizens, agencies were set up to take care of these situations and only then did the anger begin to decrease. So when the anger decreased these two sides, these two groups, were able to get to know each other and they found they didn't dislike each other at all."

Works Cited

Ashabrenner, Brent. *Dark Harvest: Migrant Farm Workers in America*. New York: Dodd, Mead & Co., 1985.

Astro, Richard. *John Steinbeck and Edward F. Ricketts: The Shaping of a Novelist*. Minneapolis: University of Minnesota Press, 1973.

Bakhtin, Mikhail. "Discourse in the Novel." In *The Dialogic Imagination: Four Essays by M. M. Bakhtin*, edited by Michael Holquist, translated by Caryl Emerson and Michael Holquist. Austin: University of Texas Press, 1981.

Bartlett, Maud O. "Wrath on Both Sides." *Forum* 103 (January 1940): 24.

Beatty, Sandra. "Steinbeck's Play-Women: A Study of the Female Presence in *Of Mice and Men, Burning Bright, The Moon Is Down*, and *Viva Zapata!*" In *Steinbeck's Women: Essays in Criticism*, edited by Tetsumaro Hayashi. Steinbeck Monograph Series, no. 9. Muncie, Ind.: Steinbeck Society of America, Ball State University Press, 1979.

Benson, Jackson J. *The True Adventures of John Steinbeck, Writer*. New York: Viking Press, 1984.

Benson, Jackson J., and Anne Loftis. "John Steinbeck and Farm Labor Unionization: The Background of *In Dubious Battle*." *American Literature* 52 (May 1980): 194–223.

Bloom, Harold, ed. *John Steinbeck: Modern Critical Views.* New York: Chelsea House, 1987.

———. *John Steinbeck's "The Grapes of Wrath."* New York: Chelsea House, 1988.

Briffault, Robert. *The Mothers: The Matriarchal Theory of Social Origins.* New York: Grosset and Dunlop, 1931.

Bulosan, Carlos. *America Is in the Heart: A Personal History 1946.* Seattle: University of Washington Press, 1973.

———. "My Education." In *If You Want to Know What We Are: A Carlos Bulosan Reader,* edited by E. San Juan, Jr. Minneapolis: West End Press, 1983.

Castro, Janice. "Labor Draws an Empty Gun." *Time* (March 26, 1990): 56–59.

Coles, Nicholas. "Democratizing Literature: Issues in Teaching Working-Class Literature." *College English* 48 (November 1986): 64–80.

Copland, Aaron, and Vivian Perlis. *Copland 1900 through 1942.* New York: St. Martin's/Marek, 1984.

Cross, George Lynn. *Presidents Can't Punt.* Norman: University of Oklahoma Press, 1977.

Ditsky, John. "The Ending of *The Grapes of Wrath*: A Further Commentary." *Agora* 2 (Fall 1973): 41–50. Reprinted in his *Critical Essays on Steinbeck's "The Grapes of Wrath,"* 116–24. Boston: G. K. Hall & Co., 1989.

———. "John Steinbeck—Yesterday, Today, and Tomorrow." *Steinbeck Quarterly* 23 (Winter–Spring 1990): 5–15.

———. "'A Kind of Play': Dramatic Elements in John Steinbeck's 'The Chrysanthemums.'" *Wascana Review* 21 (Spring 1986): 62–72.

———. "The Late John Steinbeck: Dissonance in the Post-*Grapes* Era." *San Jose Studies* 18 (Winter 1992): 20–32.

———. "Steinbeck's 'Slav Girl' and the Role of the Narrator in 'The Murder.'" *Steinbeck Quarterly* 22 (Summer–Fall 1989): 68–76.

Dobrin, Arnold. *Aaron Copland: His Life and Times.* New York: Thomas Y. Crowell, 1967.

Everest, Beth, and Judy Wedeles. "The Neglected Rib: Women in *East of Eden.*" *Steinbeck Quarterly* 21 (Winter–Spring 1988): 13–23.

Everson, William K. *The Films of Hal Roach.* Greenwich, Conn.: Museum of Modern Art, New York, 1971.

Fensch, Thomas, ed. *Conversations with John Steinbeck.* Jackson: University of Mississippi Press, 1988.

Fiedler, Leslie. "Looking Back After 50 Years." *San Jose Studies* 16 (Winter 1990): 54–64.

French, Warren. "The First Theatrical Production of Steinbeck's *Of Mice and Men.*" *American Literature* 36 (January 1965): 525–27.

———. *John Steinbeck.* New York: Twayne Publishers, 1961. Second ed. Indianapolis: Bobbs-Merrill, 1975.

Galan, Hector, and David Marash. *New Harvest, Old Shame.* Produced and directed by Hector Galan. "Frontline," WGBH-TV, April 17, 1990.

Gilligan, Carol. *In a Different Voice: Psychological Theory and Women's Development.* Cambridge: Harvard University Press, 1982.

Gladstein, Mimi Reisel. *The Indestructible Woman in Faulkner, Hemingway, and Steinbeck.* Ann Arbor, Mich.: UMI Research Press, 1986.

———. "Women in the Migrant Labor Movement." In press, *San Jose Studies.*

Goldfarb, Ronald L. *Migrant Farm Workers: A Caste of Despair.* Ames: Iowa State University Press, 1981.

Gonzales, Bobbi, and Mimi Reisel Gladstein. "*The Wayward Bus*: Steinbeck's Misogynistic Manifesto." In *Rediscovering Steinbeck: Revisionist Views of His Art, Politics and Intellect,* edited by Cliff Lewis and Carroll Britch, 157–73. Lewiston, N.Y.: Edward Mellen Press, 1989.

Greenblatt, Stephen J. "Shakespeare and the Exorcists." In *Contemporary Literary Criticism: Literary and Cultural Studies,* edited by Robert Con Davis and Ronald Schleifer. New York: Longman, 1989.

Gregory, James N. *American Exodus: The Dust Bowl Migration and Okie Culture in California*. New York: Oxford University Press, 1989.

Halladay, Terry Grant. "'The Closest Witness': The Autobiographical Reminiscences of Gwyndolyn Conger Steinbeck." M.A. Thesis, Stephen F. Austin University, 1979.

Hart, James D. "Proletarian Literature." In *The Oxford Companion to American Literature*. New York: Oxford University Press, 1983.

Hartranft, Marshall V. *Grapes of Gladness: California's Refreshing and Inspiring Answer to John Steinbeck's "Grapes of Wrath."* Los Angeles: DeVorss and Co., 1939.

Haverland, Stella. "Ruth Comfort Mitchell." Ruth Comfort Mitchell Papers, San Jose Public Library.

Higham, Charles, and Joel Greenberg. "Lewis Milestone." In *The Celluloid Muse: Hollywood Directors Speak*. New York: Viking Press, 1972.

Hoffman, Frederick J. "Aesthetics of the Proletarian Novel." In *Proletarian Writers of the Thirties*, edited by David Madden, 184–93. Carbondale: Southern Illinois University Press, 1968.

Hughes, Robert S., Jr. "A Form Most Congenial to His Talents: Steinbeck, the Short Story, and *The Pastures of Heaven*." In press, *San Jose Studies*.

Kappel, Tim. "Trampling Out the Vineyards—Kern County's Ban on *The Grapes of Wrath*." *California History* 61 (Fall 1982): 211–21.

Kramer, Mimi. "Tender Grapes." *New Yorker* (April 2, 1990): 87–89.

Levant, Howard. *The Novels of John Steinbeck: A Critical Study*. Columbia: University of Missouri Press, 1974.

———. "The Unity of *In Dubious Battle*: Violence and Dehumanization." In *Steinbeck: A Collection of Critical Essays*, edited by Robert Murray Davis, 49–62. Englewood Cliffs, N.J.: Prentice-Hall, 1972.

Lisca, Peter. *The Wide World of John Steinbeck*. New Brunswick, N.J.: Rutgers University Press, 1958. New York: Gordian Press, 1981.

Lynn, Kenneth S. "Review of 50th Anniversary Edition of *The*

Grapes of Wrath and *Working Days*." *American Spectator* (August 1989): 41–42.

McGroarty, John Steven. *History of Los Angeles County*. Chicago: American Historical Society, 1923.

McWilliams, Carey. "Did Anyone Say Steinbeck?" (letter to the editor). *New Republic* 103 (September 2, 1940): 305.

———. *Factories in the Fields: The Story of Migratory Farm Labor in California*. Boston: Little, Brown and Co., 1939.

Miller, Jean Baker. *Toward a New Psychology of Women*. Boston: Beacon Press, 1976.

Milton, John. *Paradise Lost*. In *John Milton: Complete Poems and Major Prose*, edited by Merritt Y. Hughes. Indianapolis: Odyssey Press, 1957.

Miron, George Thomas. "The Truth about John Steinbeck and the Migrants." Los Angeles, 1939. Bancroft Library, University of California, Berkeley.

Mitchell, Ruth Comfort. *Of Human Kindness*. New York: D. Appleton–Century Co., 1940.

Motley, Warren. "From Patriarchy to Matriarchy: Ma Joad's Role in *The Grapes of Wrath*." *American Literature* 54 (October 1982): 397–412.

"Movie of the Week: *Of Mice and Men*." *Life* 8 (January 8, 1940): 42.

Musmanno, Michael A. *The Story of the Italians in America*. Garden City, N.Y.: Doubleday & Co., 1965.

Nathan, George Jean. "Theatre." *Scribner's Magazine* 103 (February 1938): 70.

Owens, Louis. *John Steinbeck's Re-Vision of America*. Athens: University of Georgia Press, 1985.

Palmieri, Anthony F. R. "*In Dubious Battle*: A Portrait in Pessimism." *Artes Liberales* 3 (1976): 61–71.

Parrillo, Vincent N. *Strangers to These Shores: Race and Ethnic Relations in the United States*. 2d ed. New York: John Wiley & Sons, 1985.

Rechy, John. "El Paso del Norte." In *New Writing in the USA*, edited by Donald Allen and Robert Creeley, pp. 209–20. Middlesex, England: Penguin Books, 1967.

Roberts, Jocelyn. An unpublished paper on *The Winter of Our Discontent*.

Ruiz, Vicki L. *Cannery Women, Cannery Lives: Mexican Women, Unionization, and the California Food Processing Industry, 1930–50.* Albuquerque: University of New Mexico Press, 1987.

Sanders, Sue. "The Real Causes of Our Migrant Problem." 1940, Sue Sanders Papers, Kern County Library.

Schamberger, John. "Steinbeck and the Migrants: A Study of *The Grapes of Wrath*." M.A. Thesis, University of Colorado, 1960.

Schuster, Charles I. "Mikhail Bakhtin as Rhetorical Theorist." *College English* 47 (October 1985): 594–607.

Shedd, Margaret. "*Of Mice and Men*." *Theatre Arts Monthly* 21 (October 1937): 775.

Shillinglaw, Susan. "Carol's Library and Papers." *Steinbeck Newsletter* 2 (Fall 1988): 1–2.

———. "'The Chrysanthemums': Steinbeck's *Pygmalion*." In *Steinbeck's Short Stories in "The Long Valley": Essays in Criticism*, edited by Tetsumaro Hayashi. Steinbeck Monograph Series, no. 15, 1–9. Muncie, Ind.: Steinbeck Research Institute, Ball State University, 1991.

Sinclair, Upton. *The Jungle*. 1906. Reprint, Urbana: University of Illinois Press, 1988.

Smith, Julia. *Aaron Copland*. New York: E. P. Dutton, 1955.

Spilka, Mark. "Of George and Lennie and Curley's Wife: Sweet Violence in Steinbeck's Eden." *Modern Fiction Studies* 20 (Summer 1974): 169–79.

Stein, Walter J. *California and the Dust Bowl Migration*. Westport, Conn.: Greenwood Press, 1973.

Steinbeck, Elaine, and Robert Wallsten, eds. *Steinbeck: A Life in Letters*. New York: Viking Press, 1975.

Steinbeck, John. *Burning Bright, a Play in Story Form*. New York: Bantam Books, 1951.

————. *The Grapes of Wrath*. New York: Viking Press, 1939.

————. *The Harvest Gypsies*. Berkeley, Calif.: Heydey Books, 1988.

————. *In Dubious Battle*. New York: Viking Press, 1936. New York: Bantam, 1963, 1972.

————. *Journal of a Novel: The "East of Eden" Letters*. New York: Viking Press, 1969.

————. *Letters to Elizabeth: A Selection of Letters from John Steinbeck to Elizabeth Otis*, edited by Florian J. Shasky and Susan F. Riggs. San Francisco: Book Club of California, 1978.

————. *The Log from the Sea of Cortez*. New York: Viking Press, 1951.

————. *The Long Valley*. New York: Viking Press, 1938.

————. *Of Mice and Men*. New York: Covici-Friede, 1937.

————. *Of Mice and Men*. In *Famous American Plays of the 1930s*, edited by Harold Clurman. New York: Dell, 1974.

————. *Of Mice and Men, a Play*. In *20 Best Plays of the Modern American Theatre*, edited by John Gassner. New York: Crown, 1939.

————. Thirty-one letters to Wanda Van Brunt. September 12, 1948, to August 16, 1949. Steinbeck Center, San Jose State University.

————. *Working Days: The Journal of "The Grapes of Wrath": 1938–1941*, edited by Robert DeMott. New York: Viking Press, 1989.

————. *Your Only Weapon Is Your Work*, edited by Robert DeMott. San Jose, Calif.: Steinbeck Research Center, 1985.

Taylor, Frank J. "California's *Grapes of Wrath*." *Forum* 102 (November 19, 1939): 232–38.

————. "Green Gold and Tear Gas: What Really Happened in the Salinas Lettuce Strike." *California—Magazine of Pacific Business* (November 1936): 18.

————. "Labor on Wheels." *Country Gentleman* (July 1938): 12–13, 67.

————. "The Merritt System." *Commentator* (November 1938): 84–87. Reprinted in *Reader's Digest* 35 (February 1939): 104–6.

————. *One Story Leads to Another.* Frank Taylor Papers, Department of Special Collections, Stanford University Libraries.

————. "The Right to Harvest." *Country Gentleman* (October 1937): 7–8, 73.

————. "The Story Behind 'The Many Californias'—An Armchair Travelogue—*R.D.,* January 1952." Frank Taylor Papers, Department of Special Collections, Stanford University Libraries.

————. "Teague of California." *Country Home* (November 1935): 36.

Timmerman, John H. *John Steinbeck's Fiction: The Aesthetics of the Road Taken.* Norman: University of Oklahoma Press, 1986.

Whipple, Thomas K. "Steinbeck: Through a Glass though Brightly." *New Republic* 90 (October 12, 1938): 274–75.

Contributors

ROBERT DEMOTT

Professor of English, Ohio University, Athens, and recipient of Ohio University's graduate and undergraduate teaching awards and the Richard W. and Dorothy Burkhardt Award for Outstanding Steinbeck Criticism, Robert DeMott is also the author of several books, including *Artful Thunder* (1975), *Steinbeck's Reading* (1984), and an edition of Steinbeck's *Working Days: The Journal of "The Grapes of Wrath": 1938–1941* (1989). He has also published essays, articles, poems, and book reviews in such journals as *American Studies, Journal of Modern Literature, New Virginia Review, Ohio Review, Ontario Review, San Jose Studies, Southern Poetry Review, Steinbeck Quarterly, Western American Literature,* and *Windsor Review* and is a former chairman of the Editorial Board of the *Steinbeck Quarterly* and former vice president of the International John Steinbeck Society. He received his Ph.D. from Kent State University.

JOHN DITSKY

Professor of English, University of Windsor, Ontario, Canada, John Ditsky has published over 1,300 poems in such magazines as *New Letters, North American Review, Ontario Review,* and *Western*

Humanities Review. His poetry collections include *The Katherine Poems* (1975), *Scar Tissue* (1978), and *Friend and Lover* (1981); books and monographs include *Essays on "East of Eden"* (1977), *The Onstage Christ* (1980), and *Critical Essays on Steinbeck's "The Grapes of Wrath"* (1989). He is also the author of eighty critical articles on a variety of subjects, poetry editor of *The University of Windsor Review*, chairman of the Editorial Board of the *Steinbeck Quarterly*, and senior vice president of the International John Steinbeck Society. He received his Ph.D. from New York University.

THOMAS FENSCH

Thomas Fensch, Warner Professor of Communication, Sam Houston State University, Huntsville, Texas, is the author of *Steinbeck and Covici: The Story of a Friendship* (1979), which won the Ohioana Book of the Year Award in Biography, *Conversations with John Steinbeck* (1988), and *Conversations with James Thurber* (1989). He has also written ten other books of nonfiction including *The Sports Writing Handbook* (1988), which was a featured selection of the Writer's Digest Book Club (Winter 1989–1990). He received his Ph.D. from Syracuse University.

MIMI REISEL GLADSTEIN

Professor of English and former chair of the departments of English and Philosophy, University of Texas, El Paso, Mimi Reisel Gladstein is the author of *The Indestructible Woman in Faulkner, Hemingway, and Steinbeck* (1986) and has published articles in such journals as *College English, San Jose Studies*, and *Steinbeck Quarterly*, as well as chapters in anthologies of criticism about Faulkner, Hemingway, and Steinbeck. She served as executive director of the University's Diamond Jubilee Celebration and was a Fulbright professor of American literature in Venezuela, 1990–1991. She received her Ph.D. from the University of New Mexico.

CHARLOTTE COOK HADELLA

Charlotte Cook Hadella is assistant professor of English, Southern Oregon State College, Ashland. She has published articles in *Critique: Studies in Contemporary Fiction* and *Steinbeck Quarterly* and presented scholarly papers on Alcott, Chopin, Steinbeck, Welty, and Alice Walker at regional, national, and international conferences. She is a member of the Editorial Board of the *Steinbeck Quarterly* and was director of the MLA Steinbeck Society Meeting, 1991–1992. She received her Ph.D. from the University of New Mexico.

ROBERT E. MORSBERGER

Professor of English, California State Polytechnic University, Pomona, and editor of Steinbeck's screenplay, *Viva Zapata!*, Robert E. Morsberger is also the author of *Lew Wallace: Militant Romantic* (1980), *James Thurber* (1963), and *Swordplay on the Elizabethan and Jacobean Stage* (1974); co-editor of two volumes on American screenwriters in *The Dictionary of American Biography;* author of 150 scholarly articles, including eighteen on Steinbeck; and author of seven short stories. He is chairman of the Editorial Board of the *Steinbeck Quarterly* and received his Ph.D. from the University of Iowa.

LOUIS OWENS

Louis Owens is professor of literature, University of California at Santa Cruz, author of *John Steinbeck's Re-Vision of America* (1985) and *"The Grapes of Wrath": Trouble in the Promised Land* (1989) and co-author of *American Indian Novelists* (1985). He has written many critical articles and works of fiction and creative nonfiction; serves as co-editor of *American Literary Scholarship: An Annual;* has been the recipient of such fellowships as Fulbright, NEH, and NEA; and has received the John J and Angeline R. Pruis Award for the Outstanding Steinbeck Teacher. He received his Ph.D. from the University of California at Davis.

SUSAN SHILLINGLAW

Director of the Steinbeck Research Center and associate professor of English at San Jose State University, Susan Shillinglaw is also the author of articles on Steinbeck and James Fenimore Cooper and is currently working on a biography of Carol Henning Steinbeck. She is a member of the Editorial Board of the *Steinbeck Quarterly* and received her Ph.D. from the University of North Carolina at Chapel Hill.

THOMAS M. TAMMARO

Thomas M. Tammaro is professor of multi-disciplinary studies, Moorhead State University, Moorhead, Minnesota. He is also a widely published poet and editor of *Common Ground: A Gathering of Poems on Rural Life* (1988). He has published articles in the *Steinbeck Quarterly* and the Steinbeck Monograph Series and is a member of the Editorial Board of the *Steinbeck Quarterly*. He received his Ph.D. from Ball State University.

JOHN H. TIMMERMAN (Guest Contributor)

John H. Timmerman is professor of English, Calvin College, Grand Rapids, Michigan; author of *The Dramatic Landscape of Steinbeck's Short Stories* (1990), *John Steinbeck's Fiction: The Aesthetics of the Road Taken* (1986), and eight other books; and author of numerous short stories, poems, and critical articles. He is a recipient of the John J and Angeline R. Pruis Award for the Outstanding Steinbeck Teacher Scholar of the Year (1989) and received his Ph.D. from Ohio University.

ABBY H. P. WERLOCK

Assistant professor of American literature, St. Olaf College, Minnesota, Abby H. P. Werlock has published articles and reviews on Cooper, Faulkner, Hemingway, Steinbeck, Twain, and Wharton, as well as on gender and minority topics. She is co-author of *Tillie Olsen*

(1991) and recipient of fellowships from the NEH and the Joyce Foundation of Chicago. She received her D. Phil. from the University of Sussex, England.

TETSUMARO HAYASHI (Editor)

Professor of English and director of the Steinbeck Research Institute, Ball State University, Muncie, Indiana, Tetsumaro Hayashi is founder-editor of the *Steinbeck Quarterly* and the Steinbeck Monograph Series; co-founder and president of the International John Steinbeck Society; author and editor of twenty-nine books and twenty-two monographs on British and American literature; and author of over 100 articles on Shakespeare, Robert Greene, Steinbeck, and other literary subjects published in the United States, England, Japan, India, Poland, and Spain. He has also been the recipient of fellowships from the Folger Shakespeare Library, the Lyndon B. Johnson Foundation, the Bernard Boyd Memorial Foundation, the American Philosophical Society, the American Council of Learned Societies, and other foundations. He received his Ph.D. from Kent State University.

Index

Abbreviations:

BB	*Burning Bright* (1950)
EOE	*East of Eden* (1952)
GOW	*The Grapes of Wrath* (1939)
IDB	*In Dubious Battle* (1936)
TLV	*The Long Valley* (1938)
OMM	*Of Mice and Men* (1937)
ST	*Sweet Thursday* (1954)
WOD	*The Winter of Our Discontent* (1961)